Flash™ Web Design

the art of motion graphics

remix

  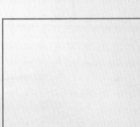 

BY HILLMAN CURTIS

New Riders

201 West 103rd Street
Indianapolis, Indiana 46290

International Standard Book Number: 0-7357-1098-8

Library of Congress Catalog Card Number: 00-111647

Printed in the United States of America

First Printing: February 2001

05 04 03 02 01   7 6 5 4 3 2 1

Interpretation of the printing code: The rightmost double-digit number is the year of the book's printing; the rightmost single-digit number is the number of the book's printing. For example, the printing code 01-1 shows that the first printing of the book occurred in 2001.

Trademarks

Warning and Disclaimer

credits

Publisher
David Dwyer

Associate Publisher
Al Valvano

Executive Editor
Steve Weiss

Development Editor
Kathy Nelson

Managing Editors
Jennifer Eberhardt
Sarah Kearns

Project Editor
Linda Seifert

Copy Editor
Daryl Kessler

Indexer
Rebecca Hornyak

Technical Editor
David Baldeschwieler

Cover Design
Todd Purgason

Interior Design
Todd Purgason
Steve Gifford

Compositors
Steve Gifford
Wil Cruz

TABLE OF CONTENTS

at a glance

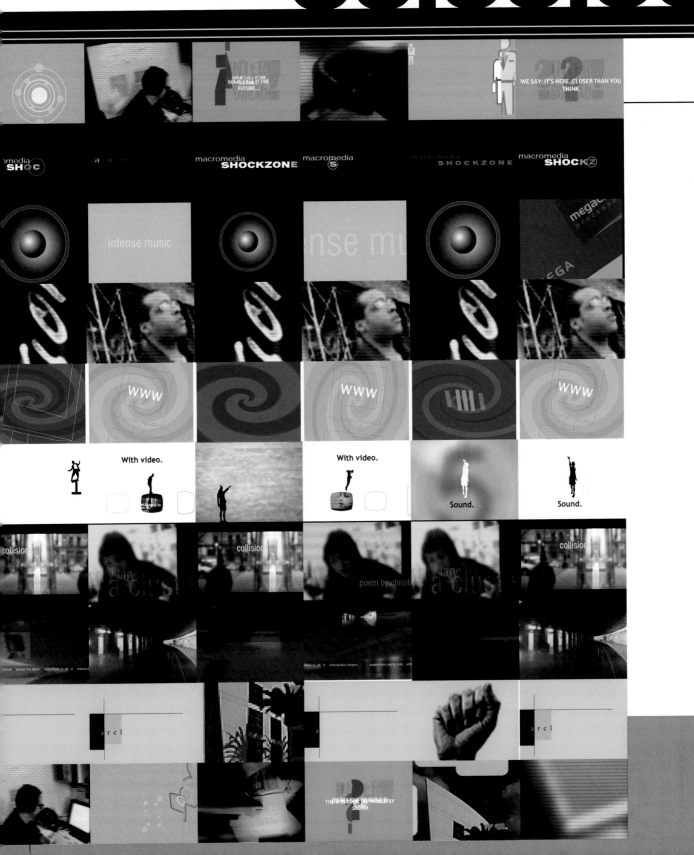

TABLE OF CONTENTS

CHAPTER 3   03:00

20k ADVERTISEMENT deconstruction

TABLE OF CONTENTS

VIDEO INTO VECTORS deconstruction

CHRISTINA MANNING POEM deconstruction

TABLE OF CONTENTS

CHAPTER 8 — 08:00

MANIFESTIVAL deconstruction

CHAPTER 9 09:00

JUXT Interactive deconstruction

CHAPTER 10 10:00

FLASH resources

INDEX 11:00

Hillman Curtis, principal and creative director of hillmancurtis.com, inc., a design firm in New York City, represents the cutting edge of motion graphic design on the web today. His expert and innovative use of Flash 4 has garnered him the Communication Arts Award of Excellence, the One Show Gold, the *New Media* Invision Bronze, and the South by Southwest Conference's "Best Use of Design" and "Best of Show." Hillmancurtis.com, his site, is a *How* magazine Top 10 web site. Hillman's work is featured in major design magazines and books, and his reputation continues to grow around the world. Hillman has appeared as a speaker at design conferences in Japan, Paris, New York, San Francisco, Chicago, and Atlanta. His company's current client roster includes Intel, Iomega, 3Com, Hewlett Packard, DSW Partners, Ogilvy One, Goodby Silverstein & Partners, SonicNet, Macromedia, Capitol Records, Lycos, WebTV, Sun, and others.

dedications

To my wife, beautiful Christina,
and my parents, Mr. and Mrs. Paul A. Zimmerman.

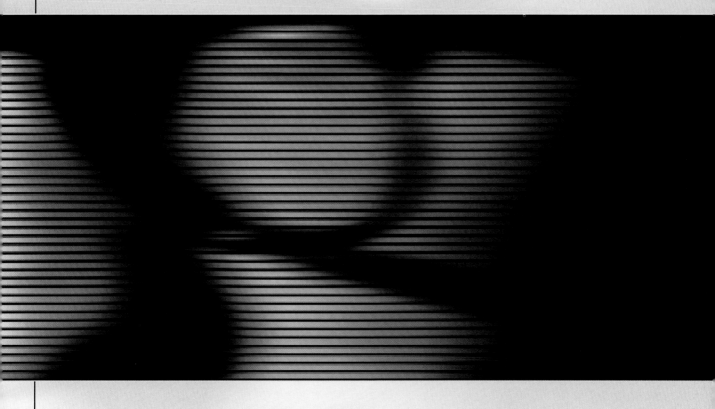

ABOUT the book
FLASH WEB DESIGN: the art of motion graphics

by HILLMAN CURTIS
designed by TODD PURGASON & Steve Gifford

ACKNOWLEDGMENTS

Hillman CURTIS

Writing this book was a team effort. My heartfelt thanks go out to the following:

Joseph Lowery, for writing this book with me. I couldn't have done it without him. (Check out Joe's upcoming books, *Dreamweaver 4 Bible*, *Dreamweaver UltraDev 4 Bible*, and the *Fireworks 4 Bible*.)

Todd Purgason, for coming in and owning the book design. Todd graced this book with his focus, passion, and exceptional gift for design, not to mention his excellent chapter contribution.

Steve Gifford, who worked with Todd and put in a superhuman effort with the layout and interior design.

All of us at hillmancurtis.com are grateful to have as our art director, Ian Kovalik. My deepest thanks to Ian for his creative and insightful chapters.

Fred Sharples hired me at Macromedia some four years ago (we're both indies now), and we've been buddies ever since. No one has the mind this guy has, and I'm honored he's shared his knowledge with me/us in Chapter 8.

Thanks to Brendan Dawes for leading this Flash 5 Remix. Thanks to Damaris Crespo and Matt Horn for technical editing this Flash 5 Remix.

And thanks to Dave Baldeschwieler and Eric Wittman, friends from Macromedia for their contributions as tech editor and author of the book's foreword, respectively.

Thanks to Homera Chaudhry for running hc.com so effectively that both Ian and I had time to give to this book.

Thanks again to Christina for proofing, re-writing, love, and support.

Also thanks to the team of Steve Weiss, Jennifer Eberhardt, Kathy Nelson, and Chris Nelson at New Riders who provided me with the perfect amount of direction, support, and encouragement.

My deepest thanks to all the good people at Razorfish NYC for their constant support and inspiration.

Thanks to Katherine Green for helping me grow as a designer, Buck Bito and all of the Macromedia Creative Services team, Matt Connors, Brian Schmidt, Rob Burgess for always saying "No gratuitous animation!", Tom Hale, Alan Felgate and all of Macromedia.

And thanks always to Mrs. John Butler, Mrs. Sears Lehmann, Rebecca Curtis and family, Madeleine Curtis and family, Joan Connors, Sarah Manning, Hugh Curtis, Garret Matoso (netfeatures.com), David Souvlewski, Dave Munro, David Hartt, Mike Davis, Brian Weisberg, David Edwards, JodyMattDonLauraEdQuentinLisaDanPaulDaveLiz CakelikeDonPiperSituationLitPlasticAutomat.

CO-AUTHORS

Todd PURGASON

My first dedication is to God as thanks for giving me this stuff called creativity and the opporunity to use it every day. Then to my beautiful wife Candice and two wonderful daughters Logan and Chloe. To my father, Jim Purgason, for teaching me how to work, and to my mother, Terrie Purgason, for teaching me how to strive for the seemingly impossible. To my company, Juxt Interactive, for the time, my partner Steve Wages for the support, and Brian Drake for pushing me to keep on my toes. To Macromedia for the great tools, and specifically to my fellow cow-tippers Brian Schmidt and Eric Wittman. To my peers that inspire and push me daily, Jimmy Chin, Josh Ulm, Brad Johnson, and too many others to mention. Finally, to the man I call a friend and an inspiration, to whom I will forever be honored and flattered by the opportunity to design his book: Thanks, Hillman; it was a blast.

Joe LOWERY

Much of life is working with the cards you're dealt and I'd like to thank the four aces who showed up for this hand: Ian, Todd, Fred, and that ace of aces, Hillman.

Fred SHARPLES

I would like to thank my father Robert, my sisters Lorna and Caroline, and my brother Raymond. Your expressions of pride, love, and support have been a great source of strength in my life and work.

I would especially like to thank my wife Pamela. Your tireless and selfless testing and editing on this chapter was the greatest help of all.

Ian KOVALIK

I would like to thank my Mother and Father for their tireless support and wisdom, my brother Adam, sister Laryn, and Grandpap Simon... also Alain, Angie, John B., Nav, Tom, Gugga, Erin, Brig, Steve, Homera, the teams at DSW and the FeedRoom—and, of course, Hillman and Christina.

Brendan DAWES

I'd like to thank my wife, Lisa, for her never-ending support and patience. Steve and the rest of the New Riders team for their unending professionalism. My family, especially my Mum and Dad for encouraging me to do what I want to do, chief cheerleader Michelle, and finally the man himself, Hillman Curtis.

ABOUT the book
FLASH WEB DESIGN: the art of motion graphics

A MESSAGE from
NEW RIDERS

Every now and then, we at New Riders happen upon a new author simply by chance. Such was the case with Hillman Curtis, who casually left his business card at a New Riders trade show booth. Hillman was interested in writing a Flash book, and we were looking to partner with the right people to create a Flash book that wasn't yet another rehash of the Flash feature set. As soon as we contacted him to find out more about his proposal, we were hooked.

Hillman is a genius in the world of motion graphics. Both technically and artistically. His software know-how, combined with his unique artistic sense, pack a powerful combination—one that we are excited to share with you in this book. You'll find that Hillman and his book are like nothing currently on the shelves. Whether you use it for reference or inspiration or both, you'll be sure to enjoy it. We'd like to know how much…

how to CONTACT US

As the reader of this book, you are our most important critic and commentator. We value your opinion and want to know what we're doing right, what we could do better, in what areas you'd like to see us publish, and any other words of wisdom you're willing to pass our way.

As Executive Editor at New Riders, I welcome your comments. You can fax, email, or write me directly to let me know what you did or didn't like about this book—as well as what we can do to make our books better. When you write, please be sure to include this book's title, ISBN, and author, as well as your name and phone or fax number. I will carefully review your comments and share them with the authors and editors who worked on the book. For any issues directly related to this or other titles:

Email: steve.weiss@newriders.com

Mail: Steve Weiss
           Executive Editor
           New Riders Publishing
           201 West 103rd Street
           Indianapolis, IN 46290 USA

Visit our web site: www.newriders.com

On our web site, you'll find information about our other books, the authors we partner with, book updates and file downloads, promotions, discussion boards for online interaction with other users and with technology experts, and a calendar of trade shows and other professional events with which we'll be involved. We hope to see you around.

email us from our WEB SITE

Go to www.newriders.com and click on the Contact link if you

- Have comments or questions about this book.

- Want to report errors you have found.

- Have a book proposal or are otherwise interested in writing with New Riders.

- Would like us to send you one of our author kits.

- Are an expert in a computer topic or technology and are interested in being a reviewer or technical editor.

- Want to find a distributor for our titles in your area.

- Are an educator/instructor who wants to preview New Riders books for classroom use. (Include your name, school, department, address, phone number, office days/hours, text currently in use, and enrollment in your department in the body/comments area, along with your request for desk/examination copies, or for additional information.)

call us or FAX US

You can reach us toll-free at (800) 571-5840 + 9 + 3567. Ask for New Riders. If outside the USA, please call 1-317-581-3500 and ask for New Riders.

If you prefer, you can fax us at 1-317-581-4663, Attention: New Riders.

technical support/ customer support ISSUES

Call 1-317-581-3833, from 10:00 a.m. to 3:00 p.m. US EST (CST from April through October of each year—unlike most of the rest of the United States, Indiana doesn't change to Daylight Savings Time each April).

You can also email our tech support team at userservices@macmillanusa.com, and you can access our tech support web site at http://www.mcp.com/support.

FOREWORD
MACROMEDIA
ERIC WITTMAN

Most viewers experience the web in a static and uninspiring manner stemming primarily from designers with limited tools for expression. The web browsing platform, as designers know it, is shifting from a medium of compromise to one where natural creations can be easily delivered. The fusing of media with emotion to effectively convey a message is a science only the savviest of designers have mastered but one everyone will need to be familiar with.

The evolution of the web medium from brochureware distribution to a continuously breathing organism is happening today through design-oriented tools and technologies. The power of Macromedia Flash allows designers to combine moving visuals, sound, and interactivity and deliver evocative content consistently to millions of people.

Through his Flash-based work, Hillman Curtis excites emotions in viewers effectively delivering life through a web browser. The techniques illustrated in this book provide insightful information on how to make functional, efficient designs using Macromedia Flash. This book is a resource every designer creating Flash content should have in his or her design toolbox.

—Eric J. Wittman
  Senior Product Manager
  Flash, Macromedia

OO:OOHOO

> "I am a designer first—that's my passion. I have a deep respect for the power of motion graphics as a tool for communication."

01:01:01

FROM HILLMAN CURTIS

I'm sitting in my small office in NYC, listening to The Arab Strap, a Scots band on Matador Records. It's summer—hot and sticky, long nights. To the right of me is a book on the video artist Bill Viola. I have tacked to the wall an image designed by the London firm The Attik and a flyer designed by Jose or one of the other fine designers at Razorfish. I'm flying out of my head on espresso and thinking about how to describe this book…its function…and its goals.

Over the last year, I have been fortunate to have established myself and my company, hillmancurtis.com, as a creative force in the small, but rapidly expanding, world of motion graphics on the web. I've done it through very hard work, but also through the development of a process—both from the standpoint of a designer, as well as someone who really understands how to get the most out of Flash. It's this process that permeates every aspect of every design we turn out here at hillmancurtis.com. It's this process that I hope to communicate with this book.

BOOK WORKS

This book contains deconstructions of several successful, real-world Flash animations and interfaces. These are files that have all been successful on the web; paid for by clients, often awarded honors. The designers have confronted and solved the type of challenges you will encounter as a Flash designer. I chose these eight files, out of the many we have designed at my shop, because they reveal most clearly the techniques that I think are crucial to becoming a successful Flash motion graphic designer.

- Chapter 2, "Deconstruction: Macromedia Shockzone," describes a Flash animation that has run on the Macromedia site for more than two years...a file that illustrates the foundation upon which I base all of my text effect animation.

- In Chapter 3, "Deconstruction: 20k Advertisement," I deconstruct an ad spot to reveal how we create immersive rich media animations with audio for the web...under 20k.

- Chapter 4, "Deconstruction: Hillmancurtis.com Navigation," explores our own navigation page, with its multi-state rollovers and video-like effects.

- In Chapter 5, "Deconstruction: 3D Wireframe," we focus on a spot where we get deep with 3D techniques and considerations.

- Chapter 6, "Deconstruction: Video into Vectors." You may have noticed this technique around the web. We take video and vectorize it, so we keep the natural movement of video and get the light file size and scalability of vectors. Very cool.

- Chapter 7, "Deconstruction: Christina Manning Poem," describes audio streaming as used in the MP3-driven *Sky*, designed to inspire as well as perform.

- I call on the programming expertise of Fred Sharples of OrangeDesign in Chapter 8, "Deconstruction: ManiFestival Site," to illustrate the foundations of smart Flash programming in a rich media site.

- I also include Chapter 9, "Deconstruction: Juxt Interactive," by Todd Purgason of Juxt Interactive, which is devoted to the unique process Todd has developed for designing for, selling to, and winning clients.

Although the book is filled with Flash tips and techniques, and includes procedures for Macromedia FreeHand 8, Adobe Premiere, Adobe Dimensions, Adobe AfterEffects, Macromedia SoundEdit 16, SoundForge, and form•Z, there is a consistent focus on design. Every chapter begins with "the thought behind the design," through which I deconstruct and reveal the concept, the design vision, and the process I used to realize success.

I am a designer first—that's my passion. I have a deep respect for the power of motion graphics as a tool for communication. If you can come away from this book with an understanding of how you can use Flash and the design process to communicate clearly, creatively, and with impact, I will have achieved my purpose here.

HILLMAN CURTIS

STRANGELOVE
HOW I LEARNED TO LOVE DESIGNING FOR THE WEB

Like many designers, I initially viewed the web as a second-rate environment…too defined by its limitations for real expression. I felt stifled by frames and tables, limited color palettes, ASCII text, and the multiple browsers and platforms that were always changing. It's a medium that can be both frustrating and intimidating, and it took me a long time to get comfortable with it. The fact is that you and I will always be challenged to change and adapt as long as we remain involved in designing for this medium. Still, something happened to me as a designer when I began designing for the web, and especially designing Flash motion graphics for the web. Those limitations, the very things that I complained about, have shaped me into the designer that I am today. I have learned to love designing for the web… and finding the possibilities within the limitations has helped me focus. I now look first at identifying the essentials—those elements that *must*, that *demand* to be included in order to communicate my message visually.

the motion is the message

Okay. What does that mean? When Marshall McLuhan theorized that "The medium is the message," he meant that the means used to communicate a message are more important and can have more impact than the message itself. Similarly, in motion graphics, the motion can be more important and have more impact than the graphic element being moved. The way you choose to move, or not move, an element across the screen can enhance the meaning of that element greatly. If, for example, I choose to move a text element slowly, scaling and fading up from black and resolving center screen, I imbue that text element with a sense of drama, focus, and, perhaps, stability. If I take the same text element and spin it around the screen, that same text takes on a sense of playfulness…or annoyance, in most cases. The point is that the motion can be your message and before I move anything across the screen I try to think about what that move is going to communicate.

motion: the universal language

Motion is a universal language. It's understood by everyone in varying degrees. Look at it this way: If something whizzes across the screen, it communicates "fast" or "urgent." And the slow move can communicate "calm." It's really about rhythm, and we all understand that language.

But, let's take it a step further. It's one thing to recognize that motion and rhythm are universal forms of communication. Fairly obvious…but communication through motion is deeply embedded in our culture in other ways. Example: Have you ever heard a movie described as being "too MTV?" The quick edits typical of music videos have become a property of the MTV brand. By establishing a particular motion-based style, MTV has added a huge attribute to its brand.

Another example would be the current Gap campaign…those slow, even pans revealing bored cynical twenty-somethings…deadpanning the songs of joy from past generations. Like 'em or hate 'em, it's all attitude, and the way the pans move says way more about Gap style, whatever that is, than the models dressed in vests and cords. Again, the end result is a corporation building brand property through motion.

In the more distinct realm of the graphic designer, motion design has even more of an influence and an impact. I can easily turn to a designer on my team and say, "This spot needs more of a Kyle Cooper look." (Kyle and his company's work can be viewed at www.imaginaryforces.com.) The designer would understand that I was looking for a darker, ominous, more distressed text approach. (Though Kyle and his company have designed film titles and commercials of many different styles, he is best known for his ground-breaking work on film titles from movies like *Seven* and *The Island of Dr. Moreau*.)

In all these examples, the content is largely irrelevant to the perceived message. It's the impact of the motion that conveys the high energy of MTV, the dismissive languidness of Gap, or the frenetic, darker style of Kyle Cooper.

moving toward a GLOBAL VISUAL LANGUAGE

The web is the first true global medium. Every web page online is available to any Internet-connected computer, anywhere in the world. Although content is often localized in a particular language, the language of the online motion graphics designer could grow to need no such translation. As designers in this new medium, we should be concerned with communicating beyond national boundaries and visualizing a global visual language, or G.V.L.

The web flows freely not only across borders, but cultures, as well. At hillmancurtis.com, about 25% of the e-mail received is from foreign countries. English is certainly not the first language of all those contacting us—and in many cases, it's not used at all—yet, the motion work that we are doing is reaching them, emotionally and meaningfully.

The challenge, then, for designers is to move toward a global visual language—that is, a language comprised of simple symbology and motion. The symbology is currently and constantly being created. A few obvious examples are the letter "e" and the "@" symbol. But others are being created and recognized as well. In the field of graphic design, the rule of designing a good logo has always been that you should be able to draw that logo in the sand. The same holds true for the symbology that will constitute, along with motion, the G.V.L.

As the web grows, other delivery platforms, such as handhelds, eTV, smart phones, and more, are being introduced. Regardless of the platform, we, as designers, need to express our message, and our client's message, with a visual language that isn't reliant on your native tongue, but is a combination of symbology and motion.

process
GLOBAL VISUAL LANGUAGE

It's one thing to formulate theories about communication; it's quite another to implement them. At hillmancurtis.com, we've developed a four-stage process, which we use to bring the theory into reality:

- Working toward a global visual language
- Respecting the technical environment
- Addressing the multitasking attention deficit
- Identifying the emotional center

As we begin to create the work, we filter every design approach through each of these four central guideposts. Each pass through our four key points hones the design more sharply and serves to keep us targeted toward the final goal.

working toward a
GLOBAL VISUAL LANGUAGE

At hillmancurtis.com, we try to move away from traditional text-based motion graphics whenever we can. Although it's not always possible or fitting—for instance, the client might have specific brand messaging required to be conveyed—major benefits are reached with a more universal approach. Many of our clients don't want to create multiple sites or interstitials (an industry term for advertisements); it's far preferable to design a site or ad that transcends cultural differences. Everyone who posts a web site has a hand in developing and defining this new global visual language. Here's a very raw example of an early adopter of G.V.L.: A site I went to by mistake consisted of a single link that read "Click here to see what I think of Ford trucks." When I clicked that link, I saw a Ford logo and an animated GIF of a beer-bellied cartoon character who then proceeded to pee on the Ford logo. Okay…pretty bad example from a design standpoint, but who is not going to understand the message anywhere in the world? I chose this as an example because it illuminates the basic principal of G.V.L.—simple universal symbology combined with motion—and it also serves to support my point that the development of this language is an organic process, an evolution that we all have a part in. Our process is to try to identify opportunities when we can communicate in G.V.L. within any given spot we might be designing.

FLASH WEB DESIGN

respecting the TECHNICAL ENVIRONMENT

It's crucial that you identify the limitations of your target market. While broadband is increasingly available across major metropolitan areas in the U.S., the 28.8 modem is still the leading conduit for the rest of the world. This narrow pipeline distinctly shapes what you can and cannot do over the web.

Even as we move into the not-so-far-flung future of viewing the web over handheld computers, or even implants, the technical environment is always going to have limitations. The online motion graphics designer has the opportunity to examine the technical environment—and respect it. The trick is to find the possibilities in the limitations and use them to your advantage. Focus on the essentials…those elements in your spot that must be there.

addressing MULTITASKING ATTENTION DEFICIT

Those of us who have worked with computers are used to multitasking. Looking at two or more programs simultaneously is the norm—while talking on the phone and surfing the web.

For example, Adam, the 19-year-old brother of hillmancurtis.com's art director, Ian Kovalik, routinely carries on several Instant Message conversations while researching topics on the Internet and listening to music through headphones. In fact, most of us, when we sit down in front of the computer, are involved in multiple tasks. The web motion designer must be aware of multitasking attention deficit (M.A.D.) and strive to present a message in a manner that will not be ignored. A piece that has all the bells and whistles with a huge "wow" factor but requires a long download does not meet this requirement. Nor does an indulgent, overwrought, or long spot (*skip intros*…as I like to call them) which I have certainly been guilty of in the past. You have to move beyond the "wow" factor to present your targeted message in 5–10 seconds. Lean and mean…kick it out. Or, in the case of Flash interfaces, not only do you need to move beyond the "wow" factor, but you have to focus on user experience. For example, I recently visited a site that offered a product I'm interested in and I couldn't navigate through the site because it had so much "wow" happening. Result: I won't be returning to the site.

identifying the
EMOTIONAL CENTER

To be a graphic designer is to be a communicator. Your vision and your message should resonate deeply—as deep as any other artistic form of expression. Yes…we are commercial artists. We make our living selling products, or events, or performer's images. Sometimes that can be difficult; nevertheless, I always try to design with passion.

The final step of the process of designing effective motion graphics is to identify the emotional center of the spot. When I sit down with clients, I train my ears to pick out words they use to describe their desires for the work. What I look for has very little to do with the storyboard, the sequence, or the verbiage. I am looking for the emotional message—it's always just one—that sums up the entire spot. It's this emotional message that I will try to communicate through motion and rhythm.

Let's look at the development of the Roger Black's Interactive Bureau spot as an example of this process.

ROGER BLACK's
INTERACTIVE BUREAU/
CIRCLE.COM
targeting the emotional center

Roger Black is one of the world's top designers. He's served as the art director for *Rolling Stone* and for *The New York Times* and is now chief creative officer of the Interactive Bureau/Circle.com. Roger is a master in communication through traditional graphic design language. His goal for the spot was to send the message that the Interactive Bureau combines the power inherent in traditional graphic design with a fluency in the latest technology.

targeting the emotional center

The first thing I do when conceptualizing is to literally draw a three-ring target. I'll do this when starting a design on my own, or while in a meeting with clients. It always ends up working the same way for me. If I am in a meeting with clients, I will draw the target and then to the side of the target I begin jotting down words that they might use when discussing the project.

When I met with members of the Interactive Bureau's creative team, I followed the same procedure. The more I listened the more I began to identify the emotional center of the spot. On my sheet of paper, next to the target I began to jot down the following phrases:

- Classic
- Solid
- Foundation
- Communication
- Latest technology
- Innovation
- Convergence
- Experience

After the meeting ended, I began to work with the words next to my target, the idea being to place one word in the center of the target and, if necessary, additional words in the outer two rings. I thought about what emotion the viewers should leave with after viewing this spot. Should they leave feeling like they just played a video game? No, that's not the intention. Maybe they should leave thinking "classic"…close. But the emotional center of this spot is much more fundamental. I can look at the Interactive Bureau and this spot and think any number of descriptives, but the bottom line and the emotional center is the word "experience"—and that's what I wrote in the center of the target.

In the second ring, I wrote "latest technology," and in the outer ring I wrote "convergence."

TECHNICAL ENVIRONMENT: identifying the essentials

The next step in my process is to identify the elements that have to be in the spot. In the Interactive Bureau spot, I had a logo element, bitmap screen grabs of some of its work, and a page of message text. The client also wanted music. All together I had a good 100–145k of essential elements. My file size limitation was set, by the client, at between 100k and 200k, provided it streamed without

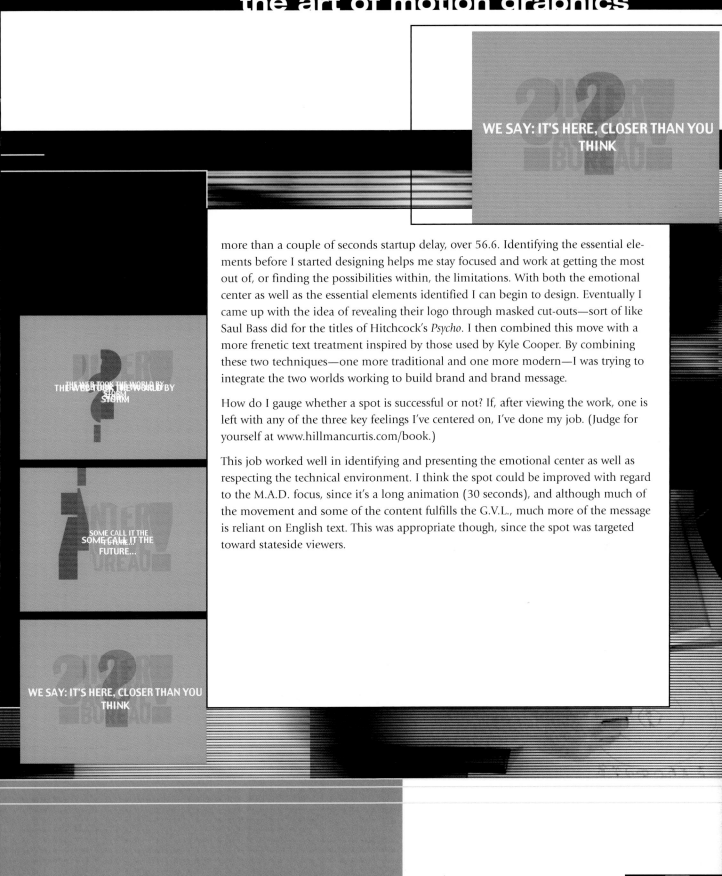

WE SAY: IT'S HERE, CLOSER THAN YOU THINK

more than a couple of seconds startup delay, over 56.6. Identifying the essential elements before I started designing helps me stay focused and work at getting the most out of, or finding the possibilities within, the limitations. With both the emotional center as well as the essential elements identified I can begin to design. Eventually I came up with the idea of revealing their logo through masked cut-outs—sort of like Saul Bass did for the titles of Hitchcock's *Psycho*. I then combined this move with a more frenetic text treatment inspired by those used by Kyle Cooper. By combining these two techniques—one more traditional and one more modern—I was trying to integrate the two worlds working to build brand and brand message.

How do I gauge whether a spot is successful or not? If, after viewing the work, one is left with any of the three key feelings I've centered on, I've done my job. (Judge for yourself at www.hillmancurtis.com/book.)

This job worked well in identifying and presenting the emotional center as well as respecting the technical environment. I think the spot could be improved with regard to the M.A.D. focus, since it's a long animation (30 seconds), and although much of the movement and some of the content fulfills the G.V.L., much more of the message is reliant on English text. This was appropriate though, since the spot was targeted toward stateside viewers.

THE WEB TOOK THE WORLD BY STORM

SOME CALL IT THE FUTURE...

WE SAY: IT'S HERE, CLOSER THAN YOU THINK

Razorfish is a leading provider of digital media content with offices all over the world. For them, the global visual language is very pertinent. I have had the pleasure to enjoy a long relationship with this company, so when they approached us with the request to help them with some early concepts for their corporate presentation, we were only too happy to help. With offices in Amsterdam, Boston, Hamburg, Helsinki, London, Los Angeles, Mannheim, New York, Oslo, San Francisco, and Stockholm, they can't really rely on big blocks of English text to communicate their message quickly across the board.

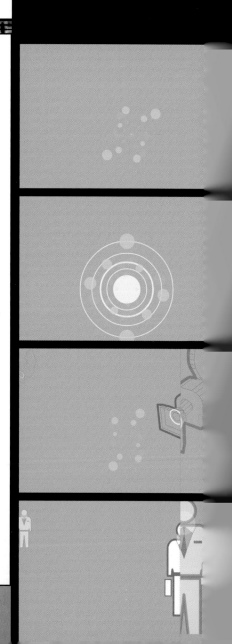

One key message for Razorfish is "Everything that can be digital, will be." This is a very complex message, not easily communicated without text. Our solution was to create a series of iconographic symbols: the house, the man, the camera, the hand, the computer, the phone. We then meshed these elements with a motion symbol we developed that served to represent "digital change." The change symbol spins and—with its motion—converts the eye icon into a camera, the camera into a computer, the computer into a handheld, and so forth.

When we showed the spot to our friends at Razorfish NY, the project manager had one key suggestion: Start the spot at a relatively slow pace and, progressively, speed it up. His reasoning was that the experience of culture in general, and his company in particular, is that digitization is growing at an exponential rate. What I thought was particularly striking about this was that his comment was pure communication through motion. Think about it…he saw the spot and added to its power to communicate, not through text, but purely through motion. The speeding up of the animation added a huge conceptual dimension to the spot. So, not only did our spot convey the message that "Everything that can be digital, will be," but it also communicated the exponential nature of this concept. This is a very simple, but very cool, example of the power of motion graphics to further amplify concepts and thoughts to enrich them further.

This spot met all four points of our process: It uses a global visual language (universal symbology and motion), respects the technical environment (12k), considers multitasking attention deficit (10 seconds), and focuses on change…exponential change…as its emotional center.

process
GLOBAL VISUAL LANGUAGE
CONCLUSION

Global visual language is happening because of our need as graphic designers to communicate. Who knows…perhaps corporate logos will be cut up and repurposed, in the same manner as hip-hop artists repurpose audio, to take on global meaning beyond their current meanings as corporate brands. But by developing a process that…at the very least…pays attention to G.V.L., technical environment, M.A.D., and the emotional center, we at hillmancurtis.com have been able to improve as designers and work toward better and more communicative motion graphics.

the art of motion graphics
of motion graphics

01:13

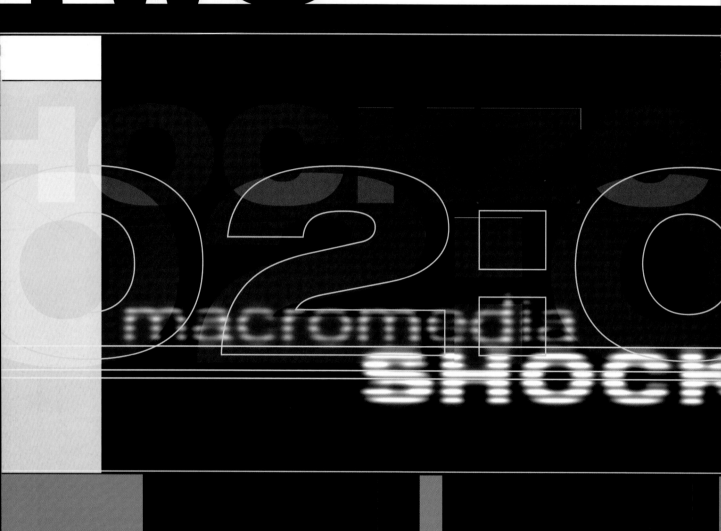

macromedia
SHOCKZONE

02:02:02

"I once had the pleasure of working with Neville Brody, the amazing British designer, who I recall saying to me (imagine a classic Brit accent), 'Hillman, It's all about consistency...consistency, consistency, consistency.'"

ZONE

a o ed a

macromedia

macromedia
SHO

macromedia **SHOCKZONE** macromedia **SHOCKZONE** macromedia **SHOCKZONE** macromedia **SHOCKZONE** macromedia **SHOCKZONE** macromedia **SHOCKZO**

02: 01

BEHIND THE DESIGN

DESIGN FOCUS
Text animation
Rhythm and pacing
Streaming
Split fades
Creating old film effects

This file, the Macromedia Shockzone, has played on the Macromedia site for over two years now. It's the longest-playing Flash animation in the history of the world…or at least it's the longest-playing Flash animation on the Macromedia site, which is still a pretty good reflection on the spot's design…or maybe just a reflection on the amount of back-work the Macromedia web team has. Either way, even after two years—an eternity on the web—the spot looks good. The design itself is based on simplicity, consistency, and functionality.

At the time of the original design, connection speeds of 28.8 weren't guaranteed. The 14.4s were still out there and CPUs were in the 100s, not the 300s of today. This Shockzone spot was designed to creatively make the most of a limited environment. That's important, because limitations will always be present in the web environment. Learning to attack these limitations creatively has always been my biggest asset when designing.

For the purposes of this design, there are a couple of key concepts to keep in mind. First, I establish a consistent language for the introduction of text. For the brand, Macromedia, I decided to bring the word onscreen one letter at a time, literally, "visually downloading" it. Rather than seeing the web's natural "streaming" as an obstacle to seamless design, I have opted to use it to my advantage by utilizing this technique. Even better, this gradual construction of text forces the viewer to focus on the word being spelled out, thus encouraging retention. Second, color, while it rarely drives my design vision, greatly enhances the intended emotional cues. As the word "Shockzone" spells on to the screen, graceful spheres of color lead the way. This lends a softness and an elegance to what is a simple, and otherwise potentially mundane, text effect.

I once had the pleasure of working with Neville Brody, the amazing British designer, whom I recall saying to me (imagine a classic Brit accent), "Hillman, it's all about consistency…consistency, consistency, consistency."

It is indeed all about consistency. Throughout the spot, each time the key word "Macromedia" and sub-phrases "Shockzone," "Shockwave," and "Flash" appear, I utilize the same effects, gradually building "Macromedia," and accenting the sub-phrase with color. In addition, I establish uniformity through the use of one font face, and a palette of seven colors (from which I do not stray!). This kind of visual consistency serves a practical purpose in terms of messaging, as well as providing the design itself with a rhythm that mesmerizes the viewer.

The only other technique I use in the spot is an effect I call the *split fade*, which is more intriguing than a typical fade to black. This is a fade that uses three instances of text or three instances of an object to fade out to black. Visualize this: The three identical instances are stacked, one on top of the other, with the topmost as the primary focus. As the topmost instance fades and recedes to black, the second and third layers split vertically, and fade out. This vertical split is a matter of five to ten pixels, up for one layer and down for the other.

Finally, I add a film grain between transitions to give the spot depth. The result is a compelling text-driven animation that uses mood, rhythm, consistency, mystery, and simplicity to keep the viewer engaged.

This example of text animation represents an essential technique in my work—that is, a focus on dynamic, rhythmic text movement. Rather than viewing the word as a static, whole entity, I try to look at each letter as having its own potential for motion. Words can break apart and spin back into place.

a   o   e   ma   o   eda   macromedia   macromedia
S!

macromedia   macromedia
SHOC   SHOCKZ

macromedia
SHOCKZONE

preparing the STAGE

This is where you set the stage size, color, and frame rate of your movie.

figure 02:01

1 Choose File > New (Ctrl-N / Cmd-N) to start a new file.

2 Choose Modify > Movie to set the Flash movie properties. When the Movie Properties dialog opens (see figure 02:01), keep the default values for a 4:3 width to height ratio. For this movie, also keep the default frame rate (12 frames per second or fps) and the default dimensions (550 pixels by 400).

The only time I change the frame rate is when I know I can afford the increase in file size and download time. The frame rate also affects streaming. If, for example, I know my target audience is using 28.8 modems, 12 fps is good because it gives my images time to stream in. For a more broadband audience, I'll raise the frame rate to 18 or 24 frames per second.

3 Set the background color to black by carefully selecting the Background color and choosing black (the first color on the standard palette).

4 Click OK.

macromedia SHOCKZONE macromedia SHOCKZONE macromedia SHOCKZONE macromedia SHOCKZONE macromedia SHOCKZONE macromedia SHOCKZONE

02:03

layers
SETUP

Flash, like many graphic design programs, is *layer based*, with the bottom layer representing the background and each subsequent layer building up from there.

I always use the same basic layers setup when starting a Flash project. Essentially, I keep all of the visual elements separate from the sound, actions, guides, and other movie components. There are good reasons for this:

- Revising completed projects is far easier when you can quickly locate the various elements, such as sound or actions. If I need to update a file months down the line, I have a clean layer setup that is consistent from project to project.

- I can pass off the file to one of hillmancurtis.com's designers—or they to me—and we will have a layer setup that is recognizable. This is a system that lessens confusion.

1 Display the Timeline by choosing View > Timeline (Ctrl-Alt-T / Cmd-Option-T). The default layer, named Layer 1, is automatically created.

2 Rename Layer 1 to "**background**" by double-clicking the name and entering in the new text. The background layer is, naturally enough, positioned beneath all other layers.

3 Create a new layer by clicking the Add Layer button (marked with a plus sign) along the bottom of the Timeline (see figure 02:02). A new layer is added above the background layer.

figure 02:02

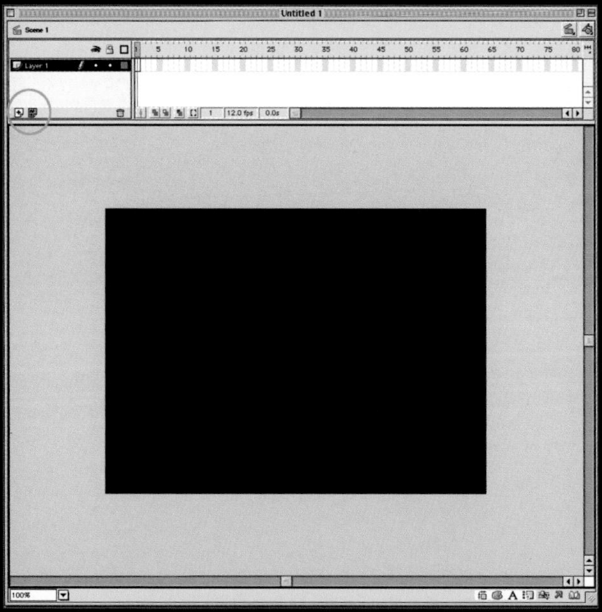

4 Repeat step 3 five more times to make a total of six layers, naming the new layers from top to bottom as follows:

labels
actions
sound (snd)
macromedia
shockzone
background

When finished, your layer structure should resemble the screen shown in figure 02:03.

figure 02:03

---

establishing a
BACKGROUND SYMBOL

Flash movies are generally intended to be viewed through a web browser, embedded in an HTML page. Consequently, your movie may be placed in an HTML page with a background color or image that works against, or clashes with, your design. For example, most of the spots I design are delivered to the client, who then adds them to his corporate site. Often, they become an addition to a preexisting page, one that has its own background color. To maintain complete control of the movie, I always create a background symbol that matches the dimensions and color of my stage.

This is extra cool because, in addition to ensuring that my background color will be present, regardless of who may be writing the embed tag, a background symbol can aid my animation. Let's say, for example, that you need to momentarily distract the viewer while bringing on a new element in your animation. With a separate background symbol, I can change the background color for a frame or two—effectively flashing the background—to draw the viewer's attention away from the new visual element, and at the same time add energy to the animation.

continues

macromedia **SHOCKZONE**   macromedia **SHOCKZONE**   macromedia **SHOCKZONE**   macromedia **SHOCKZONE**   macromedia **SHOCKZONE**   macromedia SHOCKZONE

02:05

Follow these steps to create the background symbol:

1 Click once on the background layer. The Pencil icon that appears next to the name indicates that the layer is active and ready for editing.

2 Choose the Rectangle tool from the drawing toolbar (see figure 02:04, top circle).

3 Select the Line Color button and, from the pop-up color picker, choose the No Color option (see figure 02:04, middle circle).

4 Choose the Fill Color button and select black from the Color pop-up (see figure 02:04, bottom circle).

5 Draw a rectangle over the stage. Your rectangle doesn't have to exactly line up with the stage; you'll have a chance to adjust that next.

6 While the new rectangle is selected, select the Info Panel. If the Info Panel is not visible, use the keyboard shortcut Ctrl-Alt-I / Cmd-Option-I.

7 Enter **0** in both the x and y fields. This moves the origin point of the rectangle (the top-left corner) to the upper-left corner of the stage.

8 Enter **550** in the w (width) field and **400** in the h (height) field to match the dimensions of the stage.

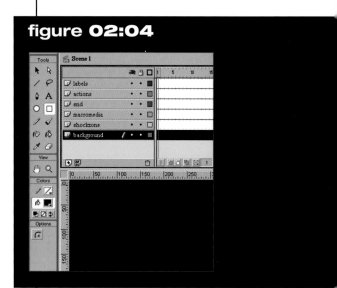

figure **02:04**

9 The selected rectangle should completely mask the stage at this point, as shown in figure 02:05.

10 With the rectangle still selected, change it into a symbol by pressing the F8 key. In the resulting Symbol Properties dialog, enter **background** for the Name and select Graphic as the behavior.

figure **02:05**

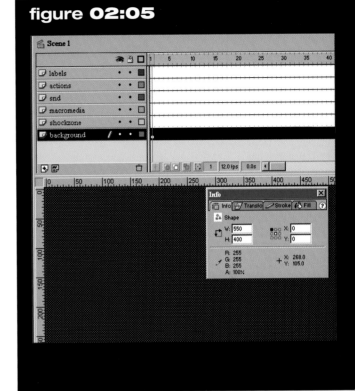

STEP 04

positioning the GUIDES

Suppose I want to create a set of guides on which to base my layout. By using Flash's Lock Guide feature, I can establish these guides and not worry about moving them. Here's a quick way to set guides.

continues

1 Click on View > Rulers and Guides > Show Guides, as shown in figure 02:06. Guides are dragged from the Ruler.

2 To create a margin around the layer, drag guides from the ruler and position them 10 pixels from the edges. For center guides, position horizontally on 200 and vertically on 275. Your guides should resemble figure 02:07.

3 Once you have all your guides in position, click on View > Guides > Lock Guides to keep them in place.

figure 02:06

STEP 05

creating the TEXT

To create the text for the initial Shockzone ad screen in Flash, follow these steps:

1 Choose Insert > New Symbol to create a new graphic symbol, labeled "macromedia." Flash automatically takes you into the Symbol Editor.

2 Select the Text tool and choose a font, font size, and color.

For the Shockzone animation, I used Vonnes Book, set at 44 points, in white. You can use whichever font settings you like.

3 Click onto the stage and type **macromedia**.

If the text looks slightly jagged, make sure that View > Antialias Text is enabled.

figure 02:07

4 Align the text to center by choosing the Align Panel. If the Align Panel is not visible, use the keyboard shortcut Ctrl-K / Cmd-K. Select the center horizontal and center vertical buttons, as well as the Align To Stage button on the right-hand side of the panel as shown in figure 02:08.

The basic text is now created, but because I want to control the rate of appearance of each letter, I need to create a layer for them all.

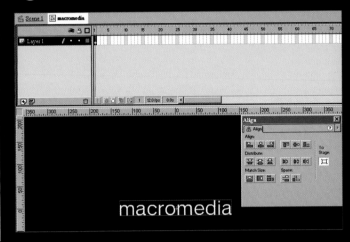

figure **02:08**

STEP 06

animating the text, PART 1

The first step in animating the text is to create the layers and break the text into individual characters that can be manipulated individually. Here's the process:

1 Create 10 layers, one for each letter in macromedia. Do not change the names of the layers yet (see figure 02:09).

2 In your initial layer, select "macromedia" and then choose Modify > Break Apart or use the keyboard shortcut Ctrl-B / Cmd-B.

The Break Apart command is used here to convert a text object into a series of shapes; the object is no longer editable as text. Our next task is to make each letter-shape a symbol and place it in its own layer.

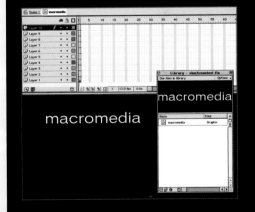

figure **02:09**

continues

3 Deselect the word group by clicking anywhere on the stage.

4 Select the first letter, m, and then choose Insert> Convert To Symbol or use the keyboard shortcut F8. In the Symbol Properties dialog, name the graphic symbol ltr-m or something similar and choose graphic as the symbol type (see figure 02:10).

5 Cut the letter using Ctrl-X / Cmd-X and select the keyframe in the topmost layer.

6 Choose Edit > Paste in Place or use the keyboard shortcut Ctrl-Shift-V / Cmd-Shift-V.

If you use the standard Paste command, Flash places the letter near the center of the stage. The Paste in Place command, on the other hand, retains the original positioning.

7 Repeat steps 4–6 for each of the remaining nine letters in macromedia.

Two notes on this process:

First, when you come to the second m in macromedia, Flash won't let you name the symbol "ltr_m" if you already have one. I add a number to indicate a different—but similar—symbol, such as "ltr_m2." The same holds true for the second a, obviously.

Second, be sure when you select the lowercase "i" to also Shift-select the dot above the letter before you cut and paste it.

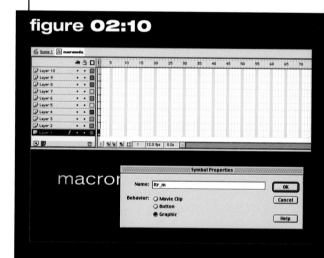

figure 02:10

8 After each letter symbol is in its own layer, name each layer accordingly by double-clicking on the current layer name and entering a new one—"**m**" for the layer that holds the letter "m," and so on. The result should resemble figure 02:11.

9 Repeat this entire operation for the word "shockzone," in a new and separate symbol called "shockzone," but this time use a Black or Bold extended font face and type in uppercase. I used Vonnes Black Extended.

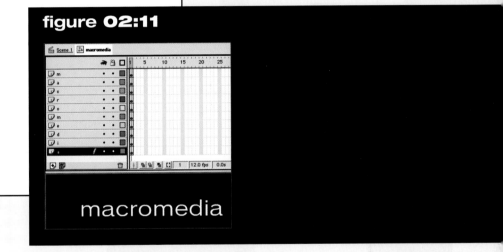

figure 02:11

media **SHOCKZON** · macromedia **SHOCKZONE** · macromedia **SHOCKZONE** · macromedia **SHOCKZONE** · macromedia **SHOCKZONE** · macromedia SHOCKZONE

02:11

adding frames and TWEENS

So far, we just have a one-frame movie—not very exciting. So now's the time to add more frames. The rhythm of the completed work depends on how long each section is given to reach completion. Rhythm makes the world go around in more ways than one…and it certainly shouldn't be underestimated in designing motion graphics. Always try to set your animation to an appropriate rhythm…whether that's a beat in your head or your audio accompaniment. For this spot, I wanted a slow, dreamlike rhythm and I worked hard to have my moves reflect that. First I added frames to, and animated, the macromedia symbol.

1 Double-click the "macromedia" symbol in the Library palette to begin editing that symbol.

2 In the 24th frame of the Timeline Inspector, select and drag down through all layers. You are essentially selecting the 24th frame on all the layers at the same time.

3 Choose Insert > Frame or press F5.

New frames are added for all the layers.

You're now ready to create the motion tween. A *tween* can be thought of as…well it probably is…an abbreviation of *in between*. In Flash, a tween is a technique that allows you to quickly animate an element over time.

4 Hold Ctrl/Cmd button drag straight down the sixth frame, through all the layers.

Note: You have to be careful that you don't accidentally drag a layer; it's best to just click once and immediately drag. If you hesitate at all, chances are you'll drag a layer or frame.

5 Select Insert > Keyframe or use the keyboard shortcut F6 (see figure 02:12).

figure 02:12

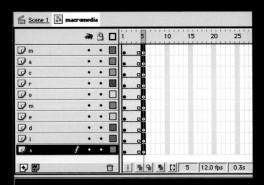

6 On the Timeline, drag straight down through all layers anywhere between the first and sixth frame.

7 Choose Insert > Create Motion Tween (see figure 02:13).

If you move the playhead back and forth across the Timeline, you won't see any change yet—but you will after the next section, when we add the fading and scaling transformations.

figure 02:13

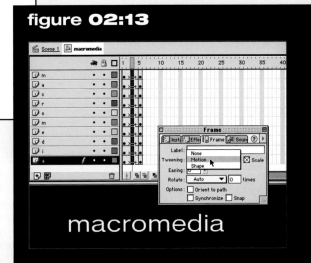

macromedia

fading and scaling
THE LETTERS

Until now, most everything has been preparation—necessary, but, I'll admit, a bit tedious. However, the advance preparation allows you to quickly and smoothly add effects and shape the animated text. As noted earlier, the "macromedia" text actually uses three different, overlapping effects:

- Each letter fades up from completely transparent to completely opaque.

- All the letters start at about 55% of their original size and grow to full size.

- Each letter appears and begins the above two tweens—and completes them—at a different time, but at the same rate.

continues

Although it seems that a lot is going on, notice how I maintain consistency in several areas. The fades all go from invisible to opaque, and the letters all scale the same amount as well as tween over the same number of frames. Only the appearance of the letters is somewhat random. Keeping the majority of factors consistent allows you to achieve interesting or eye-catching effects while still focusing on your message.

1 While still in the macromedia symbol environment, select the first keyframe in the first layer, the "m" layer.

2 Choose the Effect Panel.

3 In the Effect drop-down list, choose Alpha and lower the percentage to 0, either by entering 0 in the text field or using the slider as shown in figure 02:14.

4 With the same keyframe selected, choose Modify > Transform > Scale and Rotate or use the keyboard shortcut Ctrl-Alt-S / Cmd-Option-S to open the Scale and Rotate dialog.

5 In the Scale and Rotate dialog, change the Scale value to 55%. Click OK. Make sure the Rotate is set at 0.

6 Repeat steps 2–5 for all the layers, being careful to choose the first keyframe of each layer.

You can see the effects in action by moving the playhead back and forth. However, you'll notice that all the letters appear, grow, and become solid at the same rate. In the final steps, you'll stagger the appearance and tweening of the letters.

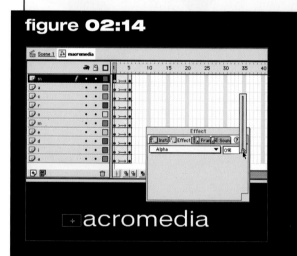

figure 02:14

7 In the first layer, highlight the range of frames between the two keyframes, inclusive—that is, from frame 1 to frame 6 (see figure 02:15).

8 Now you can drag that entire frame range to a new position in the Timeline.

9 Repeat for each layer, moving each frame to a slightly different position, until your Timeline resembles the one shown in figure 02:16.

figure 02:15

figure 02:16

omedia
SHOCKZONE macromedia
SHOCKZONE macromedia
SHOCKZONE macromedia
SHOCKZONE macromedia
SHOCKZONE macromedia
SHOCKZONE

02:15

animating the text,
PART 2

The "shockzone" element uses a different style of animation. In addition to fading up the letters—linearly, from left to right—another element is used to draw focus to each letter. As a letter becomes visible, a circle interacts with it, either growing toward it or shrinking away from it.

setting up the frames

Next you need to work with the Timeline to set up the frames for the animated text. Here is the process:

1 In the shockzone symbol Timeline, if you haven't already, apply the steps found in the previous sections "Converting Letters to Symbols" and "Adding Frames and Tweens." Your Timeline should resemble the one shown in figure 02:17.

2 Select the first keyframe in the first layer, the "s."

3 Select the Effect Panel and set the Alpha to 0.

4 Repeat steps 2 and 3 for each layer, setting all initial keyframes to 0 Alpha (transparent), but this time, scale each letter down 22%.

I wanted a slightly more subtle fade up here.

5 In the second layer (the "h"), highlight the range of frames between the two keyframes, inclusive—that is, from frame 1 to frame 6.

Figure 02:17

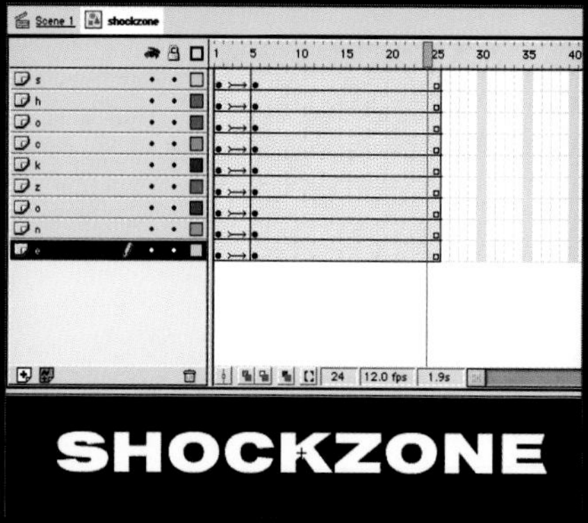

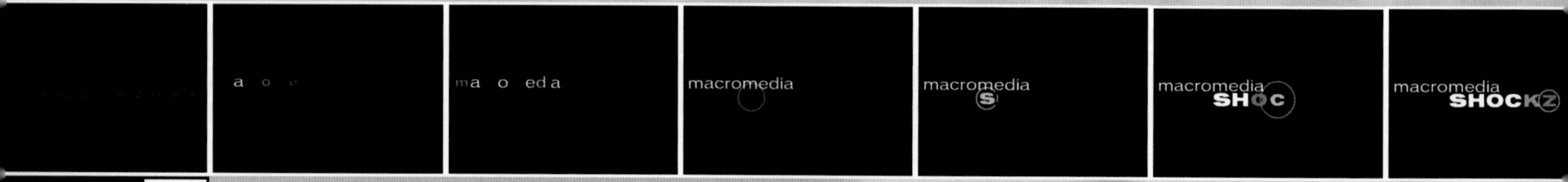

SHOCKZONE

6 Drag the frame range one frame over so that it starts on frame 2.

As you move away from the first frame, Flash automatically adds a blank keyframe at frame 1 of that layer.

7 Repeat step 5 for each layer, moving the frame range one frame higher than the frame on which the previous layer starts in a stair-step-like fashion, until your Timeline resembles the one shown in figure 02:18.

If you move the playhead across the Timeline you'll see the word "shockzone" fade up, one letter at a time across the screen, in just over one second.

figure **02:18**

creating
CIRCLES

As a motion graphic designer, I always try to keep track of how my eyes move with the spot. (I look for slight inconsistencies because I believe that these inconsistencies, no matter how small, register with the viewer.) For the "Shockzone" text animation, I decided that I needed more movement onscreen. Just fading up letters wasn't working for me, since the word "macromedia" had utilized the fade-up just seconds earlier. I came up with the idea to use circles, of different sizes and colors, to introduce each letter. This leads the eye just ahead of the letters as they fade in. The result is increased fluidity…the letters seem more liquid in their flow, and the colors of the circles, placed upon an otherwise black-and-white environment, really pop.

Along with the text, I use two circles with slightly different line weights and varied colors. Because both circles will be Library symbols, I'll be able to change the color of any instance without incurring additional file size. Naturally, I'll want to use only colors from a web-safe palette—that is, colors that appear the same in both the major browsers; the web-safe palette is standard in Flash.

1 Choose Insert > New Symbol or use the keyboard shortcut Ctrl-F8 / Cmd-F8.

2 In the Symbol Properties dialog, name the symbol **circle**.

3 Choose the Oval tool from the drawing toolbar. Behavior is Graphic.

4 Click the Fill Color button and, from the color pop-up, choose None. (see figure 02:19).

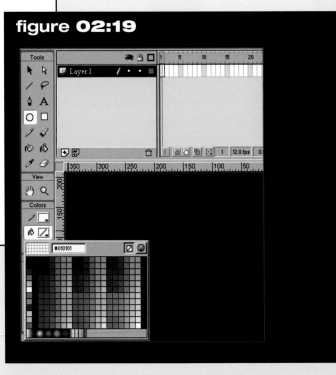

figure 02:19

5 Using the Stroke Panel, set the line width to 2. Now select Mixer Panel.

6 Select a medium green using the pencil color pop-up in the Mixer Panel.

7 In the Mixer Panel menu pop-up, select Add Swatch.

I find it very useful to make all the colors I use in each movie easily identifiable. For this reason, I always add the color I choose as a new one below the standard palette, as shown in figure 02:20.

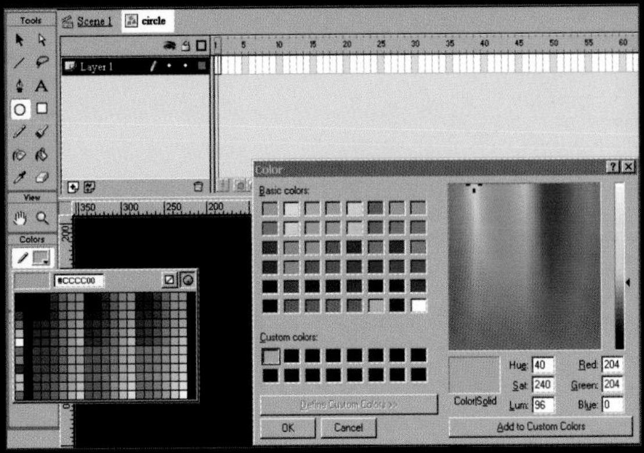

8 Draw a circle with the Oval tool by holding down the Shift key while you create the circle. Make the circle approximately 100 pixels in diameter.

You can check the size of the circle by selecting it and looking at the Info Panel. If necessary, enter new values in the width and height text fields.

9 Select the circle and choose Window > Panels > Align or use the keyboard shortcut Ctrl-K / Cmd-K, making sure to check the Align to Stage option in the Align dialog to center the shape on the stage.

10 Repeat steps 1–9 to make a second circle, with these variations:

- Name the symbol something like **circle4pt**.

- Change the line width to 4 points.

- Choose a darker green.

figure **02:20**

omedia **SHOCKZON** macromedia **SHOCKZONE** macromedia **SHOCKZONE** macromedia **SHOCKZONE** macromedia **SHOCKZONE** macromedia SHOCKZONE

02:19

combining circles AND LETTERS

Now it's time to animate. The trick here is to keep things moving smoothly enough so that the overall vibe is cool and consistent. I accomplish this by working the rhythm of the animation and varying only one or, at most, two factors, such as circle color and growth direction. The effect, hopefully, is both fluid and intriguing. The color circles lead the eye a half step ahead of the letter fade ins…it's a beautiful thing. Remember that distraction can be a powerful tool; use it to your advantage.

1 Open the "shockzone" Library symbol for editing by double-clicking on the "shockzone" symbol in the library.

2 Add a new layer by clicking the New Layer button on the Timeline Inspector.

3 Name the layer **circles** or something similar.

4 From the Library, drag an instance of one of the circle symbols onto the stage. Slide the playhead to the sixth frame so that both the circle and the "s" in shockzone are now visible, and position the circle so that it is centered over the letter.

5 Add keyframes on frames 3 and 6 and a blank keyframe on frame 7. Your time line should look like the one shown in figure 02:21.

6 Select the first keyframe and choose Modify > Transform > Scale and Rotate, or use the keyboard shortcut Ctrl-Alt-S / Cmd-Option-S to scale the circle up 125%.

Figure 02:21

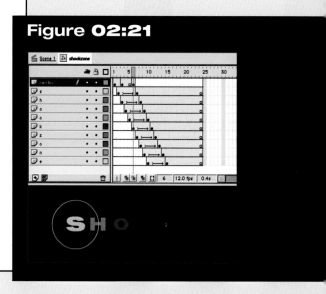

7 Select the Effect Panel and set the Alpha to 0.

8 Select the third keyframe, set its Alpha to 0%, and scale it down to 22%.

At this point you should have three keyframes of the circle. The first is larger and alpha'd out to 0, the second is in its original state, and the third is smaller and alpha'd out to 0.

9 Using the Shift key, select both frames 1 and 3.

10 Choose Insert > Create Motion Tween to tween all frames at once (see figure 02:22).

If you rewind and play this sequence, the circle will appear to zoom in on the "s" of shockzone and disappear just as the "s" is completely visible. The next step is to bring in each letter with its own circle, varying the color, circle line width, and scale.

11 Repeat steps 2–10 with the following variations:

- Use the second circle symbol: circle4pt.

- Use the Scale command to make the same circles small on the first keyframe and larger on the last.

- Change the color of the line by choosing the Tint effect from the Instance Properties dialog.

12 Continue adding a variety of circles until one exists for every letter in the word.

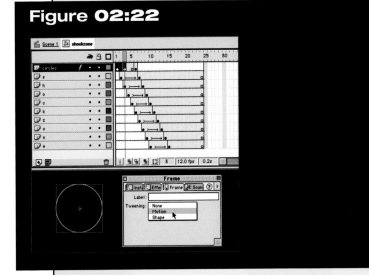

Figure 02:22

bringing it all TOGETHER

You may notice that almost all the work so far has been accomplished in the Timeline for the Library symbols rather than in the Timeline for the main stage. Working with symbols—even creating full animations—makes the final layout far easier and much more adjustable. If I built the word animations on the main stage, so to speak, and the client wants me to move each word further apart, it would be a hassle—for both of us.

The process now is to simply add the necessary frames for the total animation and to add and position the animated Library symbols.

1 On the Timeline for Scene 1, add enough frames to have 60 total frames for all layers.

2 From the Library, drag out an instance of the "macromedia" symbol onto the macromedia layer.

3 Drag the playhead across the frames until the entire word is visible.

4 Using the guides, position the word so that it is flush to the left border, slightly above the center line, as shown in figure 02:23.

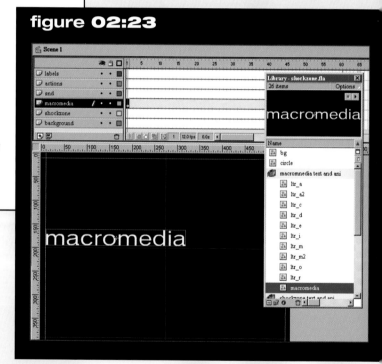

figure 02:23

5 Select the "macromedia" symbol and choose Modify > Instance and set the Instance Properties to play once (see figure 02:24).

6 On the same frame on which the macromedia animation ends, and the word is fully visible, create a keyframe on the shockzone layer.

7 Repeat steps 3-6 for the shock-zone layer, using the "shockzone" symbol and positioning it so that it is flush right and slightly below the center line. Select the "macromedia" symbol and in the Instance Panel, set the properties to Play Once.

Test your animation by moving the playhead back and forth across the Timeline or by choosing Control > Test Movie. You should see the words being animated letter by letter.

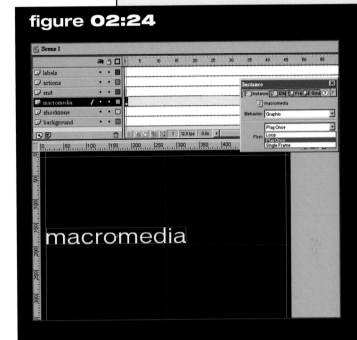

figure **02:24**

creating split fade
TRANSITIONS

Now that we have a pretty cool way to bring these words on the stage, it's time to start thinking about fading them off. Also, we need a transition to the next scene. Rather than just fade out the letters, I worked to design a unique type of transition. By inserting instances of both the macromedia and shockzone Library symbols into new layers, I can animate them in what I call a split fade. The words appear to split horizontally and fade out as they move away from the original text.

1   Add two new layers directly above the macromedia layer. Name them **macromedia-up** and **macromedia-down** or something similar.

2   Locate the frame where you want the fade off transition to begin.

     For me, the transition needed to be over fairly quickly—less than a second—and I wanted it to end the scene, so I placed the keyframe about 10 frames from the end.

3   Add a keyframe to the macromedia layer and the two new layers in the frame at which the transition is to start. You'll get a filled keyframe in the macromedia layer and two blank keyframes in your new layers, as shown in figure 02:25.

4   Select the new filled keyframe by clicking it.

5   With the new keyframe selected, hold down your Alt (Opt) key so that a small plus symbol (+) appears over the keyframe. Mousedown and drag the keyframe from the macromedia layer to the macromedia-up layer. Hold down the Alt (Opt) key while dragging a keyframe to duplicate it.

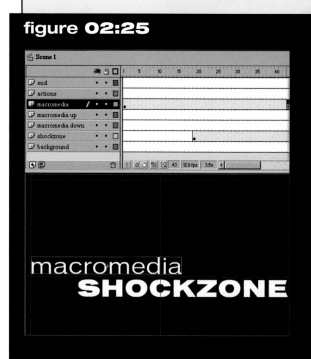

figure 02:25

6 Select the keyframe in the macromedia-up layer, choose Modify > Instance or use the keyboard shortcut Ctrl-I / Cmd-I, and set the Alpha to 80%.

7 Add another keyframe in the same layer on the second to last frame in the scene.

8 With that keyframe selected, move the macromedia text symbol up with the arrow keys so that it almost completely clears the top of the letters, as shown in figure 02:26.

9 While the second keyframe is still selected, change the Alpha to 0% by using the Effect Panel.

10 Choose Insert > Create Motion Tween to create a motion tween between the second and third keyframes in the macromedia-up layer (see figure 02:27).

11 Add a blank keyframe in the last frame of the scene by choosing Insert > Blank Keyframe or using the keyboard shortcut F7.

12 Repeat steps 6–11 for the macromedia-down layer, but move the faded symbol down instead of up.

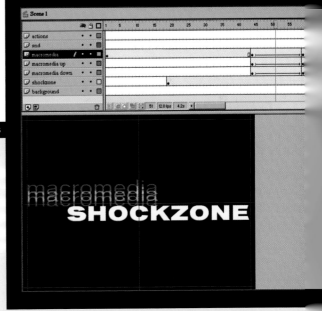

figure **02:26**

figure **02:27**

continues

13 Add a keyframe in the macromedia layer on the second to last frame in the scene.

14 While that keyframe is still selected, change the Alpha of the instance to 0 and the scale to 80%, so that while the macromedia-up and -down layers are splitting and fading, the macromedia layer is fading back.

15 Create a motion tween between the first and second keyframes in the macromedia layer.

Now, as you move the playhead across the final area of the Timeline, the word macromedia splits and fades out.

adding the film GRAIN TEXTURE

Now that the animation is almost complete, I decided to add a little more depth to the spot by inserting a film grain texture. I tried to make it look like old film scratches, but unlike real film I restrict its display to the transitions between scenes. This keeps the focus on the primary message while giving the viewer's eye more information to absorb during transitions. The repetition of the animated texture for each transition also serves to tie the various scenes together.

The film texture is made by placing small lines randomly on the stage and moving them jerkily from one place to another. I created the film scratches as an animated symbol that is dropped into a new layer and plays during the transitions.

a o o   ma o ed a   macromedia   macromedia (S)   macromedia SH○C   macromedia SHOCK(2)

To create the film scratches, follow these steps:

1 Create a new layer and a new symbol called **film scratches** or something similar.

2 In the symbol editing mode, choose the Pencil tool and a white line color.

3 Make small random lines on the screen.

4 Create four new keyframes so that there are five keyframes total.

5 In frame 2, move all the small lines away from their original position.

If necessary, choose Edit > Select All before you move the lines as a group. You can either use the arrow keys or drag the group of lines (see figure 02:28).

continues

figure 02:28

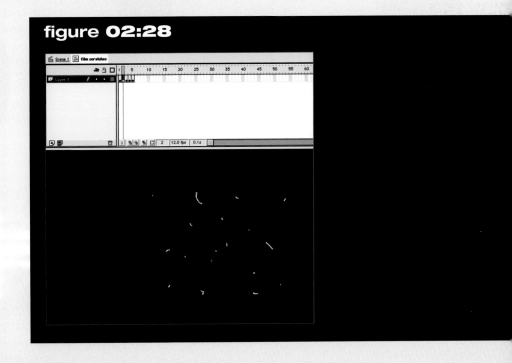

macromedia
SHOCKZONE macromedia SHOCKZONE macromedia SHOCKZONE macromedia SHOCKZONE macromedia SHOCKZONE macromedia SHOCKZONE

02:27

6 Repeat step 5 for each remaining keyframe.

7 In the Scene 1 Timeline, add the film scratches symbol to the film scratches layer.

8 Move the layer's keyframe to the first frame of the transition.

When the transition now plays, you'll get a multilayered effect by combining the split fade with the film lines and scratches texture (see figure 02:29).

All the transition textures and effects are now in place.

figure 02:29

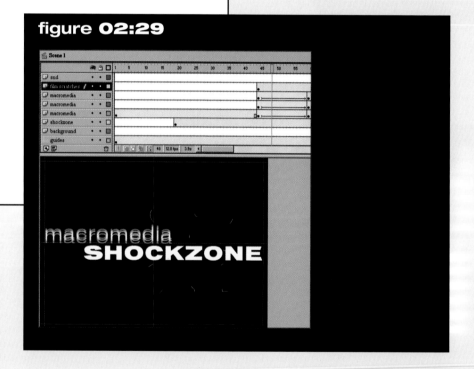

conclusion

If you love typography as much as I do, you'll start to see opportunities for motion in every word. The key is to work with restraint and emotion. This file started as a technical solution to a slow bandwidth, streaming in a letter at a time, and thus, taking advantage of the web's natural streaming. But the file grew to be more… really able to evoke a strong mood through rhythm and consistency.

 macromedia SHOCKZONE   macromedia SHOCKZONE   macromedia SHOCKZONE   macromedia SHOCKZONE   macromedia SHOCKZONE   macromedia SHOCKZONE

02:29

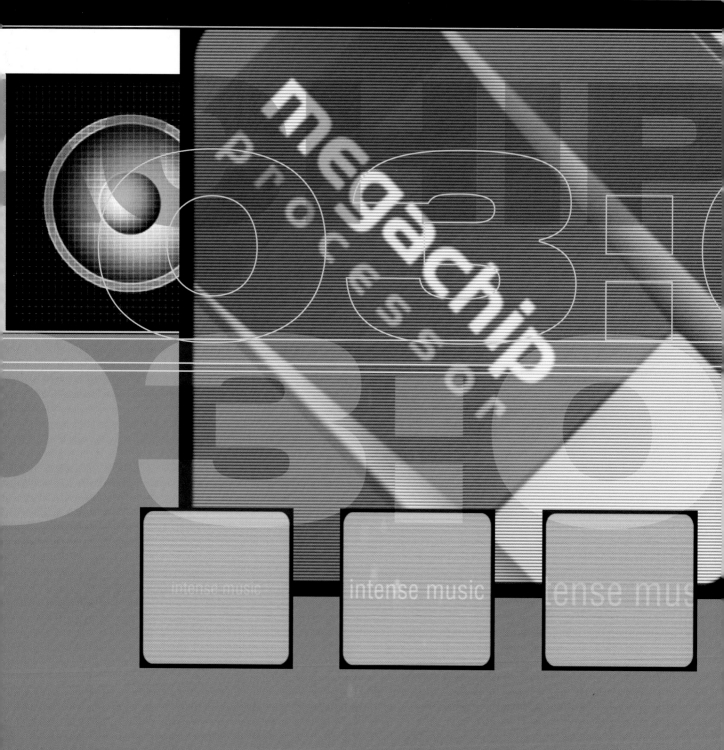

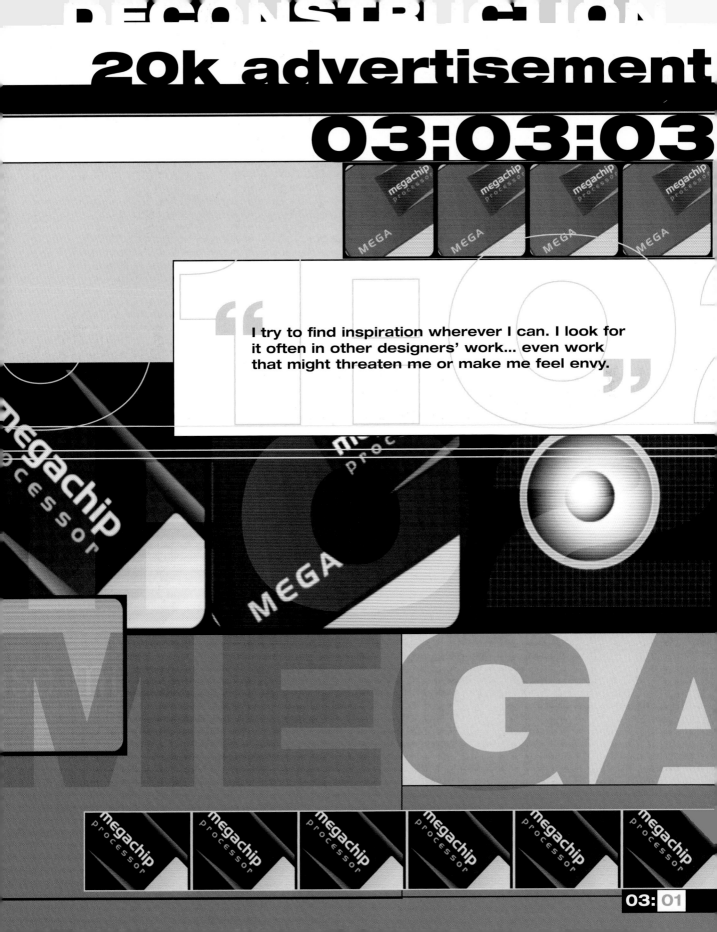

"I try to find inspiration wherever I can. I look for it often in other designers' work... even work that might threaten me or make me feel envy."

thoughts

BEHIND THE DESIGN

With this 20k Flash ad, I was presented with an interesting challenge. I was to design a 10- to 15-second spot, under 20k, with audio, using two of the client brand elements (a vector logo and a vector illustration of a computer chip) and two client message statements ("intense music" and "intense processing"). The spot was based on a storyboard that displayed the computer chip and the two message statements, and resolved with the client logo, which, if clicked upon, would jump the user to the client's main site. The vector logo I was presented with weighed in at 4k, and the computer processor chip illustration (also vector) was another 3k; that left me with about 13k to stretch over 10 seconds.

Here's how I did it:

First I identified the essentials—those elements that had to be in the spot: the computer processor chip illustration, the logo art, the phrases (message statements), and some sort of audio loop and sound effects.

Next I identified the emotional impact I thought the spot could communicate. I knew I was dealing with a chip maker that bases its business on making the fastest processors you can buy. So the first word I taped on my monitor was "fast." Also, the spot was appearing on SonicNet and Shockwave's online radio, "FlashRadio." This meant a target audience of 17 to 34 year olds. So the next word I taped up was "extreme." Finally, since the storyboard was clearly aimed at presenting the client's processor as having the power to handle "intense music," I taped up "music." I made a visual target of my words and placed "fast" in the center, "extreme" in the middle circle, and "music" in the outer circle. Because the spot's messaging says "intense music" you might think I would have chosen "music" as the central focus. Instead, I tried to get to the root of what the spot needed to communicate in order to be successful. The big picture was that the client makes fast processors that can handle a lot of audio and visual action. Emotional focus: fast.

Now that I had my focus and the essential elements identified, I was ready to go to work. The processor chip art presented a unique challenge. The chip was visually unacceptable when scaled down to fit on the stage, so I opted to present different perspectives, all magnified and all brought in with tight and quick cuts. This was successful and acceptable to the client because I carefully chose perspectives that displayed its brand. Every angle had either the client brand name, the chip model name, or both displayed. By doing this, I was able to kill three birds with one stone. I reinforced the rhythm with the quick cuts, which in turn supported my target word "fast," and I was able to display the brand. Also, by reusing one vector element (the chip), but changing its perspective, I was able to save k (file size) and keep the spot compelling.

file setup

These ads I have been producing are sized at 200 × 200 pixels and played on a number of different sites, including RealPlayer G2, SonicNet, @Home, and mPlayer. The fact that these spots are going to be passed around to several different sites justifies my insistence on creating background layers as a rule. You see, when doing client work you can't always be certain how your clients will choose to use the file…they might embed it into an existing HTML page that has the background color set to something other than that of your Flash spot. With the background layer you ensure consistent and uniform appearance.

After you've created a new file, use Modify > Movie to change both the height and width to 200. Keep the background a neutral white; we'll add our own background layer and color it black.

intense music intense music intense music nse m

First, in the Timeline, create new layers in this configuration:

guides
labels
actions
sound (or snd)
mask
chip
text
speaker
grid
background (or bg)

Also, when your movies start to get more complex and you begin to use as many layers as this one does, I suggest you reduce the height of the rows in the Timeline representing the layers. You can do this by selecting the Frame View pop-up menu and selecting Short as shown in figure 03:01.

figure 03:01

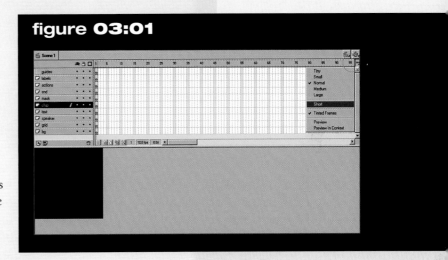

STEP 01

working with
BACKGROUNDS

This spot justifies creating background layers, and this file uses the background layer for more than just ensuring consistent appearance...I use it as a part of the animation, changing its color in flashes to add to the rhythm and excitement of the spot. This is a spot that depends on rhythm and quick cuts to convey "fast" and my background layer is a big part of the plan.

continues

setting up the background layer

This first set of steps shows you how to create and position the background rectangle:

1 Select the bg layer by clicking on it.

2 Choose the Rectangle tool from the drawing toolbar.

3 Set the line to No Color and the Fill to black (see figure 03:02).

4 Draw a rectangle over the background. With the new rectangle selected, select the Info Panel. If the Info Panel is not displayed, use the keyboard shortcut Ctrl-Alt-I / Cmd-Option-I.

5 Enter **200** in the w (width) and the h (height) fields to match the dimensions of the stage. Then enter **0** in both the x and the y fields. This will position your background square perfectly.

6 Click Apply.

7 With your bg element sized and positioned and still selected, create a new symbol by choosing Insert > Convert to Symbol (or use the keyboard shortcut F8) and name it **bg** or something similar.

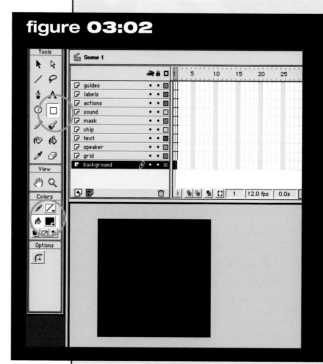

figure 03:02

STEP 02

creating a
MASK

For this spot, I use a rounded rectangle mask—a rounded window if you will—that shows the layers below it. Flash has a quick and easy way to create masks. And with Flash 5 you can mask unlimited layers. Here's how:

1 Select the Mask layer by clicking on it.

2 Double-click the Rectangle tool to display the Rectangle Tool dialog. A pop-up will appear.

3 Set the Corner Radius to 12 as shown in figure 03:03.

4 Set the line to No Color and the Fill to any color other than black and drag out a rectangle. The exact size, shape, and position of the rectangle doesn't matter. Nor, for that matter, does the color, since this is going to be a mask. I use the Object Inspector to specify all those values.

figure 03:03

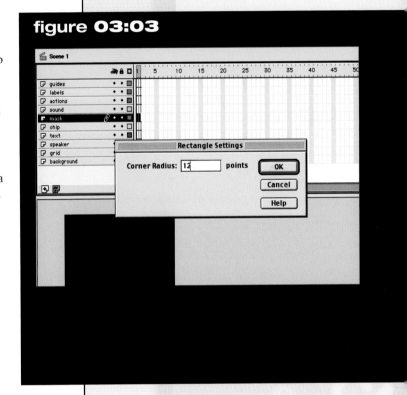

continues

5

Select the Info Panel. If the Info Panel is not displayed, use the keyboard shortcut Ctrl-Alt-I / Cmd-Option-I.

With the rectangle (now with rounded corners) selected, enter the following values in the Object Inspector:

x: 5
y: 5
w: 190
y: 190

6

With your mask element sized and positioned and still selected, create a new symbol by choosing Insert > Convert to Symbol or use the keyboard shortcut F8 and name it **mask** or something similar.

Your completed mask should resemble the one shown in figure 03:04.

7

Now, double-click on the page icon of the mask layer. In the pop-up that appears, choose the Mask option (see figure 03:05).

Your next step is to define which layers you want to be masked—in other words, which of the elements you want to show through the beveled window defined by the mask.

8

Double-click on the page icon of the layer directly below the mask layer—in this case, the chip layer. In the pop-up, choose Masked.

A shortcut to this step is to hold down the Ctrl-Alt / Cmd-Option keys and click the layer.

figure **03:04**

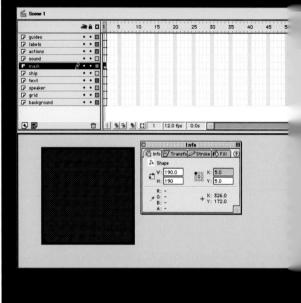

figure **03:05**

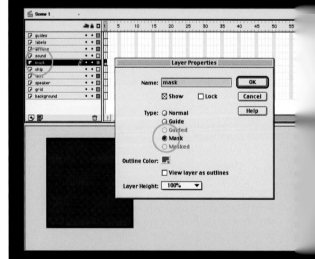

   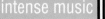

intense music   intense music

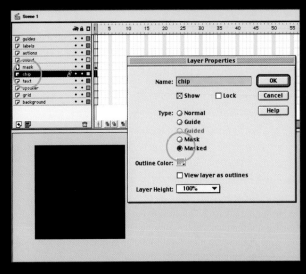

figure 03:06

9 Mask all layers below the mask layer (see figure 03:06).

To activate the masking effect, all layers (the mask and those masked below it) must be locked, which can be done by clicking the lock icon in the layers (see figure 03:07). I usually wait to do this until much of the animation is complete. I change the mask layer to outline view by clicking on the Outline icon in the mask layer (see figure 03:08). This allows me to see the boundaries of the mask as well as the layers below it.

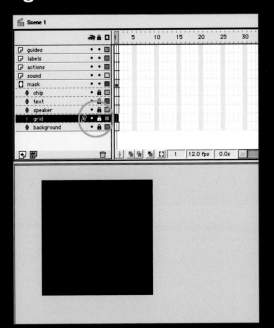

figure 03:07

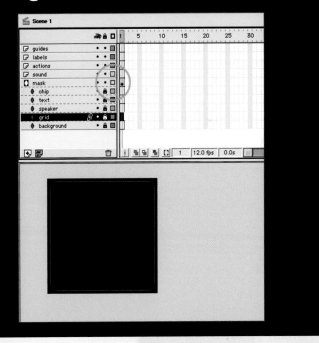

figure 03:08

designing the grid ELEMENT IN FREEHAND 8

I try to find inspiration wherever I can. I look for it often in other designers' work...even work that might threaten me or make me feel envy. One such designer that has me pretty pumped lately is Klaus Mai, author of "007 Design Agent." Mai and his company KM7 use a lot of grids as background elements and I took that as the inspiration for the background grid element in this spot. In fact, I get a lot of inspiration from print designers and that leads me to Macromedia FreeHand. Traditionally known as a leading print and illustration tool, FreeHand has been adding web-authoring features that actually make sense.

In this chapter you'll use FreeHand to quickly create, and export to Flash, perfect grid elements. I should mention that you don't have to use FreeHand. If you are comfortable with another, similar product, such as Adobe Illustrator, that's fine. In fact, you don't have to use any other tool in conjunction with Flash, but my goal when I started this book was to share my secrets...and my techniques...and if I left out FreeHand, I would be leaving out a tool that has really helped me realize many of my design visions.

figure 03:09

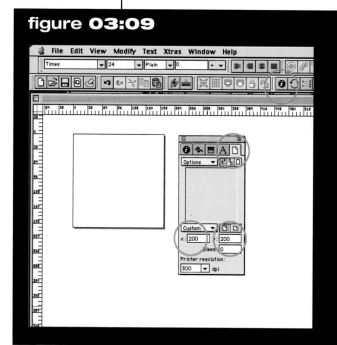

1 In FreeHand, open a new document. Select File > New and, using the Object Inspector, set the document size to 200 × 200—exactly the same as your Flash document size (see figure 03:09).

figure 03:10

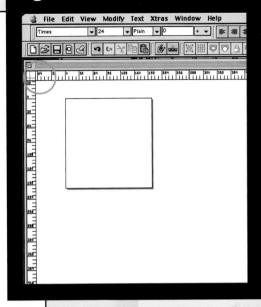

2 If not already visible, enable the rulers in FreeHand by choosing View > Page Rulers. Drag the zero-point marker (the cross-hair in the intersection of the vertical and horizontal rulers shown in figure 03:10) to the upper-left corner of the page in the document window.

3 Use the Line tool to draw a single horizontal straight line.

4 Choose Edit > Clone to duplicate the line in place.

5 Use the down-arrow key to move the cloned line 10 pixels below the original line.

6 Choose Edit > Duplicate or use the keyboard shortcut Ctrl-D / Cmd-D. The duplicated line appears 10 pixels below the cloned line.

7 Repeat step 6 until you have enough duplicated straight lines to fill the stage (see figure 03:11).

Now that the horizontal lines are complete, it will take just a few more steps to add the vertical lines and complete the grid.

8 Choose Edit > Select All.

9 With all the lines selected, choose Modify > Group.

10 Choose Edit > Clone.

figure 03:11

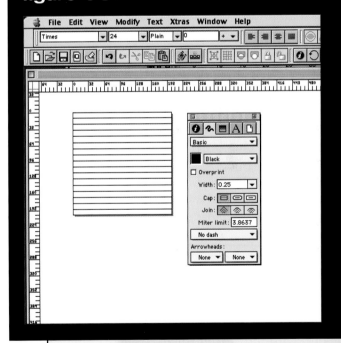

continues

STEP 03 continued

11 Choose Modify > Transform > Rotate and enter **90** in the Rotation Angle field (see figure 03:12).

The cloned horizontal lines become vertical and the grid is complete.

12 Choose File > Export and select the Flash (*.swf) file type.

13 Enter a file name (**grid**) and click Save when you're done.

figure 03:12

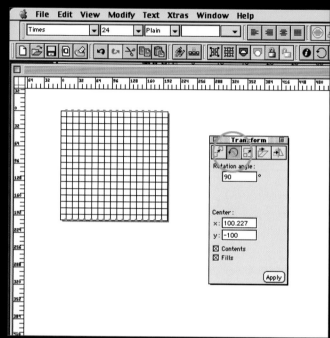

STEP 04

importing the grid INTO FLASH

Importing your FreeHand files into Flash is a breeze. Macromedia makes both Flash and FreeHand and has worked overtime to make sure the two complement each other.

1 In Flash, create a new Library symbol called grid by choosing Insert > New Symbol or use the keyboard shortcut Ctrl-F8 / Cmd-F8.

continues

intense music   intense music tense mus nse m

STEP `04` **continued**

2 While in edit symbol mode, import the exported grid.swf that you exported from FreeHand earlier by choosing File > Import or using the keyboard short-cut Ctrl-R / Cmd-R.

3 Group the elements by selecting all of them, choosing Edit > Select All, and then choosing Modify > Group. Next, center the elements on the page using the Align command. Choose Modify > Align or use the keyboard shortcut Ctrl-K / Cmd-K. Make sure to check the Align to Stage option in the Align dialog.

4 Return to the Movie Editor, choose Edit > Movie, select the Grid layer, and drag from the Library an instance of the grid symbol.

5 Center the grid symbol on the page using the Align command.

STEP `05`

adjusting the GRID

As it currently exists, the grid symbol is just a grouped set of black lines, invisible on the stage—we want to make sure these lines are hairline in width and white in color. Here's how:

1 Double-click the grid symbol in the Library to enter into editing mode.

2 Choose Edit > Select All.

3 Select Modify > Break Apart, or use the keyboard shortcut Ctrl-B / Cmd-B, twice.

Breaking apart ensures that the grid is in line form—you need to do it twice.

continues

4 Choosing the Stroke panel allows you to change both the line thickness and the color.

5 Change the Line Thickness to hairline by choosing that value from the drop-down list.

6 Choose white from the color pop-up. The grid should resemble figure 03:13.

Next, adjust the grid's Alpha in your Movie Editor. This will blend the grid back a bit so it's not so obvious, instead becoming a subtle background element that adds to the depth of the spot but won't distract from the foreground elements.

7 Return to the Movie Editor by selecting Edit > Edit Movie.

8 Select the grid by clicking on its keyframe in the grid layer.

9 Choose Modify > Instance or use the keyboard shortcut Ctrl-I / Cmd-I and in the resulting Instance Properties pop-up, select the Color Effect tab.

10 Select Alpha from the drop-down menu and lower the Alpha to 20.

At this point you can check how the grid will look when masked. Simply click on the Lock/Unlock All layers icon at the top of the layer window to lock all layers.

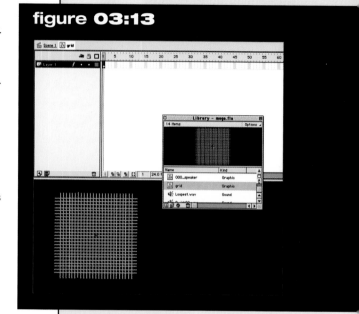

figure **03:13**

intense music intense music tense mus nse m

STEP 06

designing with GRADIENTS

A *gradient* is a smooth blend of two or more colors. Flash applies excellent gradients that can be used to give graphics a three-dimensional appearance. The speaker graphic used in the 20k example uses two gradients: one for the inner and one for the outer cones. Flash offers complete gradient editing control and you can use that control to build both concave- and convex-appearing objects.

Before you can apply the gradients, you must first create the speaker outline that will hold the gradients.

1 Create a new Library symbol called speaker. Select Insert > New Symbol or use the keyboard shortcut Ctrl-F8 / Cmd-F8.

2 While in the symbol edit environment, choose the Oval tool, set the line to Gray and the Fill to no color, and drag out a circle. Press Shift while dragging to constrain the oval to a circle.

3 Use the Info Panel to set the width and height of the circle to 125.

4 Select the circle and center align it using the Align command, again making sure to check the Align to Stage option in the Align dialog.

5 Copy the circle and paste it in place using Edit > Paste in Place. This will paste the copied circle exactly on top of the first.

Paste in Place is a very valuable asset; it basically pastes the object on the stage in the same position (or at the same x,y coordinates) as it was copied from.

continues

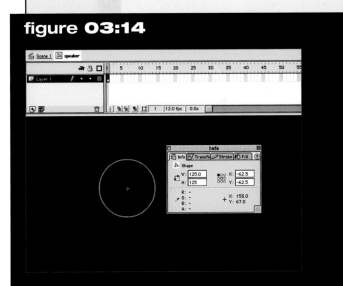

figure **03:14**

6 Choose Modify > Transform > Scale and Rotate and scale the pasted circle to 40% of the original. You'll need to scale and rotate this newly pasted circle before ever deselecting it, or you'll wipe out the original beneath it.

The final outline forms a border about the speaker.

7 Select Paste in Place again.

8 Scale this third pasted circle to 110%.

The resulting graphic should resemble the speaker outline shown in figure 03:15.

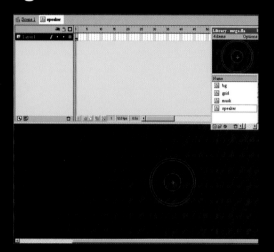

figure **03:15**

STEP 07

fleshing out the speaker
USING GRADIENTS

figure **03:16**

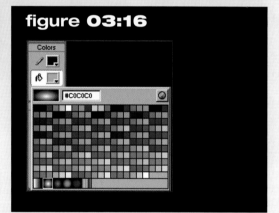

Gradients are a fill type and are thus available through the Paint Bucket tool. Although you can create your own gradients, the default black-to-white radial gradient is perfect for the speaker.

To apply the gradients for a 3D look, follow these steps:

1 Choose the Paint Bucket tool and, from the Swatch Panel, select the radial gradient (second from the left at the bottom) as shown in figure 03:16.

2 Fill the innermost circle with the gradient.

Although the gradient is close to what I am ultimately looking for, some adjustment is still required. Flash offers a Transform Fill tool for just that purpose.

continues

3 While the Paint Bucket tool is still selected, choose the Transform Fill tool, and select the just-filled gradient. The Transform Fill tool appears at the bottom right of the toolbar; it will appear only when you select the Paint Bucket as shown in figure 03:17.

The gradient editing handles appear around the selected gradient as shown in figure 03:18.

4 Adjust the gradient as necessary by manipulating the gradient editing handles.

I increased the gradient's scale handle, as shown in figure 03:19. This caused the hotspot of the gradient to soften a touch.

5 Apply a second gradient to the middle circle.

6 Select Transform Fill modifier again.

A general rule of user interface design holds that for any three-dimensional object, the light source should come from the upper left of the screen. To make one area appear to bulge out of the screen (convex) and the other to appear to recede (concave), I'll adjust the outer gradient so that the center point is opposite that of the inner gradient.

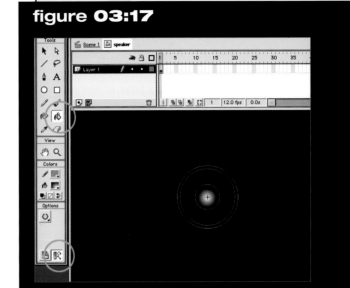

figure **03:17**

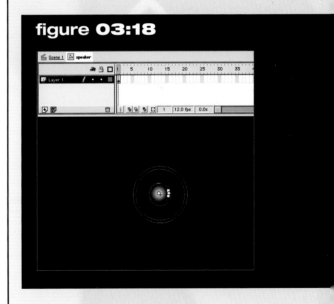

figure **03:18**

continues

7 Complete the speaker by filling the area between the outermost and the middle circle with a medium gray. Other modifications can be made to finish the speaker, such as changing the color of the innermost circle's outline to a light orange to define it better, and/or removing the outermost line.

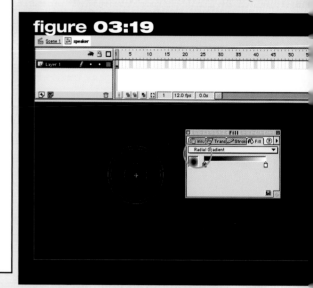

figure **03:19**

STEP **08**

animating the
SPEAKER

My goal with the speaker is to create a rhythm that is going to communicate "fast." If I animated the speaker with the traditional tweening methods, I'd end up with smooth motion that doesn't necessarily convey my message. Moreover, tweens are processor intensive on the user system. I developed a technique that utilizes blank keyframes to create quicker cuts from one frame to another, which works well in this situation. It's faking tweens to get a bit more pop.

To animate the speaker, follow these steps:

1 Return to the Movie Editor. Select Edit > Edit Movie and in all layers add approximately 50 frames by click-dragging down through the layers at frame 50 and choosing Insert > Frame or using the keyboard shortcut F5.

2 In the speaker layer, create a blank keyframe by choosing Insert > Blank Keyframe or using the keyboard shortcut F7 on frame 5.

continues

intense music intense music tense mus nse m

3 Making sure the blank keyframe on frame 5 of the speaker layer is still selected, drag an instance of the speaker symbol from the Library onto the stage.

4 Center the speaker on the stage using the Align command.

5 Make a keyframe by choosing Insert > Keyframe or using the keyboard shortcut F6 on frame 7. With the Modify > Transform > Scale and Rotate command, scale the speaker down to 60%.

6 Make another keyframe on frame 9, and remove transform by selecting Modify > Transform > Remove Transform. This will return the speaker to its original size. Now, lower the Alpha setting to 45 by using the Effect Panel, and choosing 'Alpha' from the effect type drop down.

I use the Alpha modification to vary the appearance of the speaker so that it doesn't become too predictable.

7 Make a final keyframe on frame 11, scale the speaker up 110, and restore the Alpha to 100.

8 Add a blank keyframe immediately after the first three existing keyframes in the speaker layer (on frames 6, 8, and 10). Add a final blank keyframe on frame 13 as shown in figure 03:20.

The addition of the blank keyframes after the speaker appearances makes for a quicker cut...more pop...of the speaker element. We're establishing a rhythm that should jolt the viewer's attention. Quick and fast...like a drum beat. After this sequence, I leave the speaker onstage, static, for a few seconds so that it will overlap the next element to appear...the text.

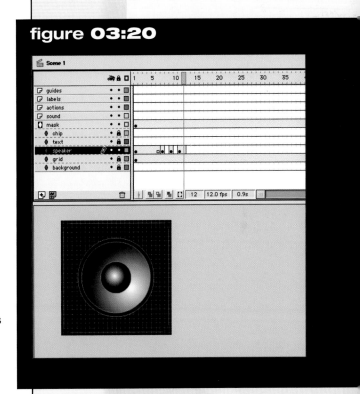

figure 03:20

adding text and
making use of
CONTRASTING RHYTHM

If you watch this spot in action, you might notice a contrasting rhythm. The speaker and the chip quick-cut like crazy but they are separated by slow and steady fade ups of the text. This is fantastic to me. I love to play with pace like this. This sort of subtlety can get me pretty worked up because, let's face it…if I kept quick-cutting everything in the entire spot, it might appeal to a spider monkey on crack, but it would fly by most of us as yet more empty "wow" design. You can flash colors and spin stuff all you want, but my goal is to always try and move beyond the "wow" factor.

1   Create a new Library symbol called text01.

2   While in the symbol edit mode, select the Text tool and type **intense music**. Choose white from the color palette and use the Helvetica font at about 24 points.

3   As always, center your text using the Align Panel. And, as always, make sure to select the 'To Stage' button on the right of the panel.

4   Return to the Movie Editor (select Edit > Edit Movie or use the keyboard shortcut Ctrl-E / Cmd-E).

5   Place a blank keyframe by choosing Insert > Blank Keyframe or using the shortcut F7 in frame 11 of the text layer. Drag an instance of text01 from the library to the stage and center using the Align command (see figure 03:21).

6   Add a keyframe (using the shortcut F6) in frame 17 of the text layer.

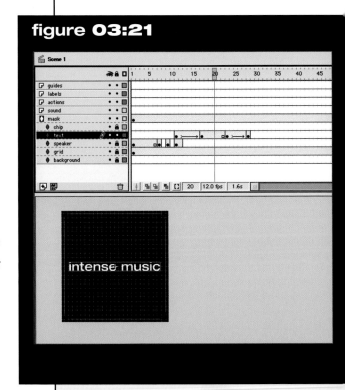

figure 03:21

intense music   intense music   tense mus nse

7 Tween the two frames by clicking any of the frames between them and selecting the Frame Panel. From the tweening drop-down menu, choose 'Motion'. This will tween, or interpolate, any differences between the keyframe in frame 11 and the keyframe in frame 17. At this point, nothing would happen, simply because both keyframes are identical. You'll apply differences in the following steps.

8 Select the first keyframe (frame 11) and use the Modify > Transform > Scale and Rotate command to scale the text down to 30%.

9 Now lower the Alpha setting to 0 through the Effect Panel.

10 Add keyframes (using the shortcut F6) to frames 23 and 28 and tween them.

11 Select the keyframe in frame 28 and scale it up, then alpha it down to 0.

12 Add a blank keyframe (using the shortcut F7) in frame 29. Your Timeline should resemble the one shown in figure 03:22.

Try playing the animation. First, rewind it by choosing Control > Rewind or use the keyboard shortcut Ctrl-Alt-R / Cmd-Alt-R. Now, choose Control > Play or simply press your Enter key. You should have a quick-cut sequence of the speaker, which leads to the fade up of the text. The text will then sit on the stage for a second and burst off, fading up and out. This is cool because it gives the viewer a chance to read the message while at the same time establishing a contrasting rhythm in the spot. Also, try playing around with your frame rate...bump it up to 18 by choosing Modify > Movie.

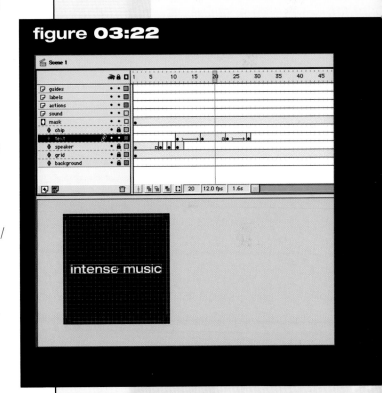

figure 03:22

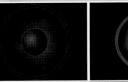

using CLIENT ART

Quite often, a client has established a brand and developed logos or images to be used in an advertisement. By and large, client art cannot be altered in any way. For Flash, it's important that the client art be delivered to you in vector format. Vectors are generally very light and they redraw cleanly at any resolution. The client art for this ad—a final logo and a processor chip—was created in Adobe Illustrator (see figure 03:23).

Although Flash can import and use Illustrator files directly, I often find it useful to open up the files in FreeHand (you can use Illustrator too) and clean them up a bit, first. It's not unusual to find numerous unnecessary layers and/or poly-gons used in the construction of the image that can be removed without altering the look. The more of this you can uncover and delete, the lighter the object will be and the better it will animate. You have to figure that the computer has to redraw everything, so if your object has 20 layers of extraneous junk, the computer will still have to redraw that stuff, which translates to a slower redraw/heavier file. Always think lean and mean. File clean-ups are a time-consuming, tedious process, but one that's well worth the effort. (I actually get pleasure from it…but that's a subject better left to me and my therapist.)

figure 03:23

In this case, the processor chip art was particularly problematic. Not only were there many layers of extraneous stuff, but the chip itself was approximately 350 pixels wide by 160 high. Remember that our stage is only 200 × 200, so there's no way that the chip could be seen com-pletely without being heavily reduced in scale. Reducing it to that small a size meant I would lose the chip's brand and model name…they would be too small to see clearly. (Not to mention the chip looked pretty bad at that small a size.) To maintain the spot's focus and keep the brand as visible as possible, I decided to present close-up views of sections of the chip throughout the ad. To keep the look dynamic and somewhat unpredictable, I varied the angles of the artwork, carefully choosing my views so that one of the brands was always clearly visible, without being cropped in any way.

intense music | intense music | tense mus|nse

1 Insert a new Library item by choosing Insert > Create New Symbol and naming it **chip** or something similar.

2 In the symbol editing mode, import the client art (select File > Import or use the keyboard shortcut Ctrl-R / Cmd-R).

3 Align to the center of the page by using Modify > Align.

4 Return to the movie editing mode (select Edit > Edit Movie or use the keyboard shortcut Ctrl-E / Cmd-E).

5 In the chip layer, create a new keyframe at frame 28.

6 Drag an instance of the chip symbol onto the stage.

I use the Scale and Rotate tool (Modify > Transform > Scale and Rotate) to position the chip at a size and angle that displays the company's brand and the product name, as shown in figure 03:24.

But, I am confronted with a problem. The chip is lost in the black background. No problem; I'll just change the background color. This will kill a couple of birds with one stone because it will add punch to this section of the spot and provide visual distraction that helps me cut to the chip. It's sort of like thinking more like a film editor for a moment rather than an animator....

7 On the bg layer, create a new keyframe (use the shortcut F6), also on frame 28.

figure 03:24

continues

8 Select the keyframe and choose the Effect Panel.

9 From the Effect Panel, choose tint from the drop-down list.

10 Select a bright green color from the pop-up menu and change the Tint Amount to 100%.

This works pretty well—so well, in fact, that I decided to reinforce rhythmic consistency by changing the background color when the text is introduced as well.

11 On the bg layer, create a new keyframe (use the shortcut F6) on frame 13 and tint it light gray.

Notice how this improved the flow of the spot. We are "cutting" between three scenes: the speaker, the text, and the chip.

Continuing with the chip animation…

12 In the chip layer, create a keyframe (use the short-cut F6) in frame 31.

13 With that keyframe selected, set the Alpha to 60 using the Effect Panel.

14 Create another keyframe, in the chip layer, at frame 33.

15 With that keyframe selected, scale and rotate the chip almost 90 degrees and scale it up so that the product name is big and clear, as shown in figure 03:25.

figure 03:25

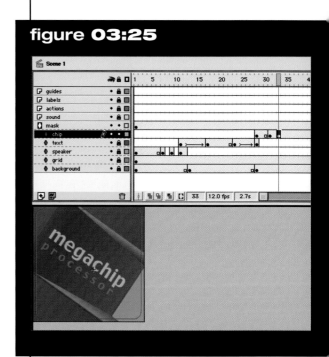

intense music intense music tense mus nse

16 Create another keyframe in the chop layer, at frame 36, and lower the Alpha setting to 60 using the Effect Panel.

17 Add blank keyframes at frames 32 and 37 by pressing the F7 key. Your Timeline should resemble the one in figure 03:26.

This is what I mean by faking tweens. By setting up a rhythmic series of views of the chip, I am able to convey "fast," while not stressing the CPU and always reinforcing the client brand. Not only that, but I am able to creatively reuse one element (the chip) over a good amount of the spot, reducing my need for other elements and, thus, lightening my file size. Again, I worked hard to find the possibilities within the limitations.

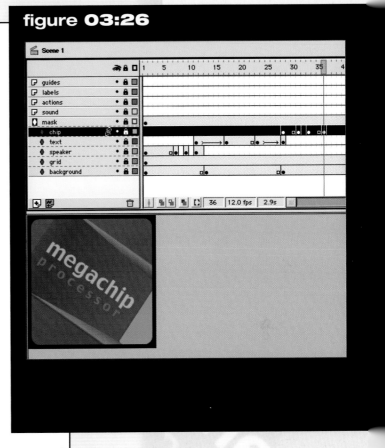

figure **03:26**

adding SOUND

What's motion graphics without sound? Well…it's motion graphics without sound. Some spots really don't need sound. If you are building an interface, it can be annoying to have sound every time that interface loads, or some drum beat looping incessantly while the user tries to concentrate on choices. But…when designing traditional motion graphics—ad spots, film titles, interstitials—sound is fantastic.

I often use two or more overlapping sounds: a looping audio clip that lays down a bed of background music and a non-percussive sound effect. Why non-percussive? It's relatively difficult to sync a sound exactly with a graphic in a Flash file. The playback is going to vary from machine to machine, depending on the CPU speed. If I used—say, a kickdrum, or a clipped boom or bang sound to introduce an element on stage—I would most likely never be assured of synchronization from one machine to the next. By using a softer, less definite sound…in the case of this ad and many of my other spots…such as a swoosh, or whooshing sounds, I minimize the sync problem. The swoosh is going to sound appropriate if it starts as the element is introduced or after it has been introduced or even while it's being introduced. (There are sync solutions in Flash, covered in Chapter 7, "Deconstruction: Christina Manning Poem," but these solutions require that I choose to stream my audio, and that often means frames are dropped in favor of a smooth audio stream. That wouldn't work for this spot.)

To work with sound, you'll need to use an audio editor like Sound Forge on the PC or Sound Edit 16 on Macintosh. Shareware waveform editors are also widely available. I start with royalty-free sound loop libraries as well as sound effects libraries. For drum loops, try any of the hip hop or "drum loop" CDs you can find at music stores…look for a place

that's selling electric guitars and keyboards and they should have them…or try any of the many loop sites online. I like http://www.loopz.com.

You can digitize the music or sounds off the CD directly into your audio editor.

With loops, once you've sampled the audio, you need to find the most appropriate start point and end point for your loop. This is largely a trial-and-error procedure where the goal is to find the smallest bit of music that loops cleanly, without obvious breaks. The loop should be short, but not so short that it's annoying. One trick that I use to make sure I'm on the beat is to pay attention to the high hat rather than the snare or kick drum.

With sound effects, you need to use a slightly different technique. Sound effects libraries are available on the web: Hollywood Edge (www.hollywoodedge.com) is a little expensive but well worth it; The Daily Wav (www.dailywav.com) and wav.com offer limited effects for free. Again, I know that I can't always guarantee an absolute sync between the visual and the auditory, given the wide range of Internet connections and machine CPUs available, so I avoid percussive sound effects and go for those with longer attack and/or release.

Another rule I follow with all audio samples is to always export them at their native rates. If a sound was originally sampled at 44mHz, for example, export it from the audio editing program at the same rate. Flash has a terrific compression engine and this method ensures that your loops and effects are at their highest possible quality when they come into Flash. Finally, always remember that with Flash on Windows systems, use .wav files and with Flash on Macintosh systems, use .aiff files for audio.

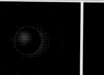

intense music intense music tense mus nse m

To incorporate a sound loop and effect in your Flash movie, follow these steps:

1   Rename the snd layer as **sound loop** or something similar.

2   Insert a keyframe at frame 5.

3   Choose File > Import and locate your looping audio file.

4   Click on the keyframe and select the Sound Panel.

5   In the Sound Panel, select the looping file name from the Sound drop-down list.

6   Leave the Effect at None and set the Sync to Start, as shown in figure 03:27.

7   Enter a relatively high number, like 99, into the Loops text field.

Flash doesn't have an infinity setting, so you need to enter a number higher than the movie is intended to play.

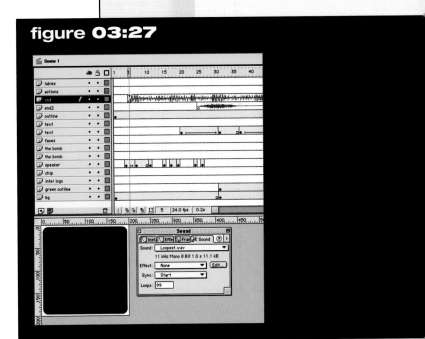

figure **03:27**

continues

8

Create a new layer for the sound effect and repeat steps 2–7 to set up the effect with these variations:

- Place the keyframes aligned with the appearance of key elements, such as the chip.

- Import the sampled sound effect.

- In the Frame Properties, leave the Loop setting at 0.

Suppose that when you are playing your file back, the drum loop—which you looped 99 times—continues to play even though your file has stopped playing. The answer is to set the Sync setting to Stop.

9

Add a blank keyfame (use the shortcut F7) where you would like the sound loop to stop.

10

Click on the keyframe and select the Sound Panel.

11

Select the looping file name from the Sound drop-down list and choose Stop from the Sync settings (see figure 03:28).

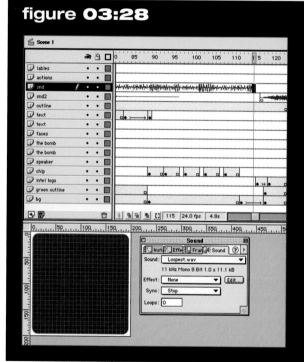

figure **03:28**

intense music   intense music tense mus nse m

STEP 12

optimizing sound
FOR THE WEB

Sound adds a lot to Flash movies but, like bitmaps, sound can create very large files for even the shortest amount of time. In the highly restricted environment of online advertising, almost every media asset must be optimized, balancing file size and quality. Flash has excellent compression capabilities, but you must take the time to use them to get the best overall effect. (Chapter 7 goes deeper into third-party tools and techniques for audio editing and enhancing.)

compressing audio
in Flash

You can compress audio in two places in Flash. First, you can set the overall compression defaults through the Publish Settings feature, accessed via File > Publish Settings, which applies a global compression to the sounds in your movie. This is a good choice if you have one sound, or several sounds from the same source. Second, you can optimize each file independently through the Sound Properties dialog accessible from the Library. This is good if you have many different sounds, because you can vary the compression for optimal file size and audio quality. I'll use the latter method for this file….

1 Double-click on the sound in the Library to open the Sound Properties dialog.

You can also select the sound and then choose the Information symbol along the bottom of the Library.

2 In the Sound Properties dialog, shown in figure 03:29, note the current compression settings and file size displayed next to the waveform image. You can test the audio quality—what the audio sounds like at this compression—by clicking the Test button.

figure 03:29

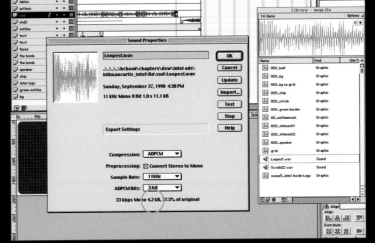

continues

3
From the Export Settings Compression drop-down list, select ADPCM.

Why ADPCM? Normally I would reserve ADPCM for short sound effects and use the far superior MP3 compression for music and voice-overs. However, my client specified that this file needed to be compatible with the Flash 3 player, and MP3 compression is available only with the Flash 4 player.

4
Select the Test button to hear your sample with the current settings.

5
If desired, select the Convert Stereo to Mono option.

Unless you're using a stereo effect, such as panning from left to right, select this option. Converting to mono reduces your file size.

6
Select a lower Sample Rate and/or lower ADPCM Bits.

7
Select the Test button again to judge the acceptability of the sound using the new compression settings.

8
Try different compression settings until you find the one with the smallest file size that maintains an acceptable quality. Click OK when you're done.

intense music intense music tense mus nse m

preloading for
STREAMING

With a series of actions, you can preload a good part of your file so that the rest will stream, hopefully, without a glitch.

I use the same basic preload technique for almost all my files. Flash has a preload code included, but it has to be set up properly. In essence, here's what my preload action does:

- Checks to see whether a particular frame has been loaded.

- If the frame has not been loaded, continues preloading assets.

- When the frame—and all the desired assets included up to that frame—have been loaded, begins playing.

NOTE   I use labels, thus the "labels" layer in all of my file setups, rather than frame numbers because it's far easier to adjust your timing with them. You can just drag the label keyframe to a new location rather than reopening the Frame Properties dialog and altering the code.

Here are the steps for establishing the preload for the spot:

1   In the label layer, click the blank keyframe in frame 1.

2   Select the Frame Panel, and in the Label text field, enter home.

A label named home is inserted. Click Insert > Keyframe or use the keyboard shortcut F6 to insert a keyframe on the next frame to label.

3   Repeat steps 1–2 on frame 4 to create a label named "start."

continues

4 Repeat steps 1–2 on frame 25 to create a label named "load" (see figure 03:30).

5 In the action layer, double-click the keyframe in frame 1 to open the Frame Actions Panel.

6 From the list of actions on the left of the panel, click on 'Basic Actions' to display all the simple actions. From the list, drag the 'If Frame Is Loaded' action into the script window on the right.

figure **03:30**

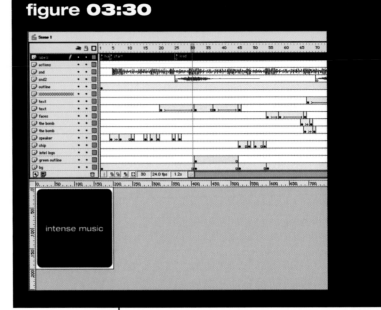

The If Frame Is Loaded script is written into the script window as shown in figure 03:31.

7 Press Ctrl-N / Cmd-N to make sure you are in 'Normal Mode' for the script window. Choose 'Frame Label' from the Type drop-down list, and choose Load from the Frame drop-down on the right-hand side of the panel.

Now you need to tell Flash what to do if the frame you specify has been loaded.

figure **03:31**

8 Double-click on the Go To action. The Go To action should be added to your script between the If Frame Is Loaded curly brackets.

9 Make sure the Go To and Play option is checked at the bottom of the panel, as shown in figure 03:32.

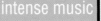

intense music intense music tense mus nse

10 Choose Frame Label from the Type drop-down list and choose Start from the Frame drop-down list (see figure 03:32).

11 For this action to work properly, another loop must be added.

12 In the actions layer, add another keyframe to frame 2 and double-click it to open the Frame Actions Panel.

13 Add a Go To action and specify the home label. Be sure to enable the Go To and Play option. This creates a loop that sends the playhead back to the script in frame 1, until that script returns a positive.

Imagine your computer talking to itself : "No, frame 'load' is not cached…I'll go to and play frame label 'home'…" The computer is forced to ask the question again and stays in this loop until the answer is "Yes, frame 'load' is cached…now I'll go to and play frame label 'start'."

figure 03:32

Now that a preload loop has been established, you can easily adjust what gets preloaded by moving the "load" label from one frame to another. If the label is on the same frame as another element's keyframe, such as a sound effect, that element—and all the elements inserted prior to that one—will be loaded.

using the bandwidth PROFILER

How do you tell how effective your preload script is? Flash includes a utility called the Bandwidth Profiler for just such a purpose. The Bandwidth Profiler allows you to set the bandwidth most applicable. Moreover, both the streaming and the movement of the playhead can be viewed together so that you can quickly gauge whether an adjustment is necessary. The Bandwidth Profiler also gives you a great deal of detailed information about your movie: its file size, duration, and even the preload time—a very important factor.

1 Choose Control > Test Movie.

Flash generates an .swf file and plays it within the authoring environment.

2 Press Enter (Return) to stop the movie.

3 If necessary, select a new modem setting from the Control menu.

4 Select Control > Rewind to make sure you're at the start of your movie.

5 Choose View > Bandwidth Profiler or use the keyboard shortcut Ctrl-B / Cmd-B.

Flash draws a bar graph depicting the streaming assets. Elements that appear above the red line indicate a problem, where the assets weigh more (the file is bigger) than the streaming can comfortably support.

6 Select View > Show Streaming or use the keyboard shortcut Ctrl-Enter / Cmd-Return.

As the movie plays, the green indicator bar shows the state of the streaming, whereas the playhead indicates which frame is being played (see figure 03:33). Ideally, you want the streaming indicator to be just ahead of the playhead at all times, while invoking the shortest preload time possible. Avoid situations in which the playhead catches up to the stream and must wait for more material to load.

7 If necessary, return to the Flash Movie Editor and adjust the placement of the preload loop (in this example, the "load" label) and then repeat steps 1–6 to retest the movie. The idea is to minimize the time spent preloading and still guarantee a smooth playback.

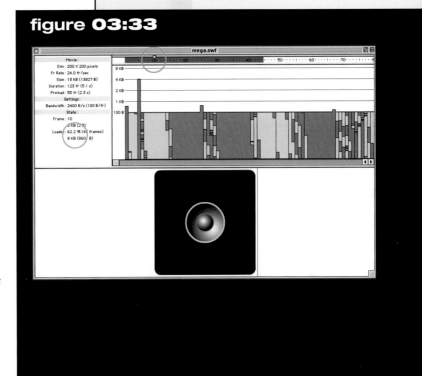

figure 03:33

STEP 15

using the SIZE REPORT

If you find yourself in a position where you're not reaching your goal—the file is not streaming properly, it's too big…or maybe, God help you, you even start considering putting a "file loading" bar on the front of the file—you need to identify the assets that are causing the most problem and work to reduce their size. The tool that I use in this situation to further optimize my movies is the Size Report. The Size Report is generated when the Flash movie is exported.

continues

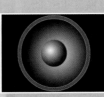

The Size Report is a text file that holds several key bits of information:

- A frame-by-frame listing of the bytes used

- The fonts, letters, and number of text bytes used

- The Library symbols used and their size in bytes

- Each sound and bitmap, including a listing of the size of each and their size after compression

To create the Size Report, follow these steps:

1 Choose File > Export Movie.

2 From the Export Flash Player dialog, select the Generate Size Report option, as shown in figure 03:34.

Get in the habit of always selecting the Protect from Import option—especially with commercial files. When this option is enabled, the file cannot be downloaded from the web and deconstructed.

This protects both my work and my client's proprietary assets. Also note that I chose to export as Flash 3 as per my client's request. Had I used MP3 and chosen Flash 3 here, a warning box would have appeared informing me that MP3 was not supported in Flash 3.

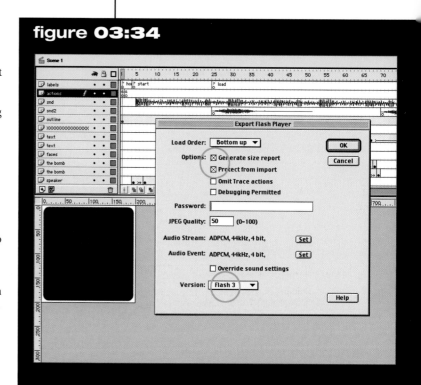

figure **03:34**

3

In any text editor, open the file *myMovie* Report.txt, where *myMovie* is the name of the file you exported. Notice there is a frame-by-frame record as well as a gauge of what each symbol, sound, and font family is costing you in file size (see figure 03:35).

```
                              mega.swf Report

Movie Report
------------

Frame #   Frame Bytes   Total Bytes   Page
-------   -----------   -----------   -------
   1          638           638       Scene 1
   2           15           653          2
   3            2           655          3
   4          280           935          4
   5         4206          5141          5
   6           22          5163          6
   7           17          5180          7
   8            2          5182          8
   9            2          5184          9
  10            2          5186         10
  11            8          5194         11
  12            6          5200         12
  13            2          5202         13
  14            2          5204         14
  15           18          5222         15
  16            6          5228         16
  17           18          5246         17
  18            2          5248         18
  19           11          5259         19
  20          743          6002         20
  21           22          6024         21
  22           22          6046         22
  23           22          6068         23
  24           38          6106         24
  25         1601          7707         25
  26           38          7745         26
  27           26          7771         27
  28           22          7793         28
  29           22          7815         29
  30           22          7837         30
  31          120          7957         31
  32            2          7959         32
  33            2          7961         33
  34            2          7963         34
  35            2          7965         35
  36            2          7967         36
  37            2          7969         37
  38           22          7991         38
  39           22          8013         39
  40           22          8035         40
  41           22          8057         41
  42           22          8079         42
  43           23          8102         43
  44           23          8125         44
```

conclusion

You have to admit there are some pretty cools things covered here—working with masks, faking tweens for speed, working with gradients and audio, as well as a good look into Flash's optimizing and testing tools. But it's the rhythm—the film/video cutting language we got going here—that floats my boat a bit higher, if you know what I mean. Establishing that kind of visual consistency and beat is a joy, both to create and to watch. The spot did indeed clock in at less than 20k...18k to be exact...and DSW partners (my client) was psyched.

04:04:04

> " My lack of ability in the area of vector illustration combined with my love of film and film titles pushed me in a bitmap-driven, cinematic direction with Flash. Although I have since learned to work the vector tip, this cinematic direction remains a huge part of my style. "

BEHIND THE DESIGN

When I was writing this book, I was going through the beginning stages of a hillmancurtis.com site redesign. In a few months my beloved, original navigation buttons would be history. However, they served me and countless visitors well, and remain an excellent example of multiple state rollovers and how to work with movie clips. Also, they provide a good introduction to the utilization of sequential (video) bitmaps.

Although my navigation page is somewhat minimal in design, it's a design based on smart interactivity. I wanted interactivity that was justified, that deserved to be there. If I was to have rollover states they were going to have to communicate. For example, for the Up state of the button I chose lopped video clips—taken largely from small sections of film leaders and film edit effects—which worked perfectly because they were beautiful and looped seamlessly. I decided I wanted to use small, quick-loading examples of motion throughout the site. I wanted visitors to see and understand that hillmancurtis.com was a company devoted to expression through motion graphics. For the Over state of the button, I chose a video of an eye opening. As it is, when the mouse is rolled over a button, the film leader loop disappears and is instantly replaced by the video of an eye opening. On both rolloff and mousedown, the eye closes and the film effects return. I wanted a button rollover that was visually compelling and that communicated to the viewer the underlying message: "Take a look."

To realize my design vision, I used a series of different programs to prepare the material and then brought it all together in Flash. Preliminary layout was done in FreeHand where I once again created a mirror document and guidelines as covered in Chapter 2, "Deconstruction: Macromedia Shockzone." For the video I used Adobe Premiere to export a series of sequential bitmaps that I then manipulated in Adobe Photoshop.

DESIGN FOCUS

Multi-state rollover navigation buttons
Working with "video"
Working with movie clips
Using the Tell Target action
Optimizing and testing the file

NOTE

Although this chapter goes into detail about Adobe Premiere, the technique and logic I demonstrate with Premiere will work with any digital video editing program that can export bitmaps. The important thing to grasp is the concept: to present what looks like video in Flash by using individual, sequential stills exported from the video itself.

movie CLIPS

For this navigation button I use movie clips instead of animated graphics like the previous examples. The primary difference between a movie clip and an animated graphic is that, whereas animated graphics work with the main Timeline, a movie clip uses it own Timeline. This means that regardless of what is happening on your main Timeline, the movie clip will be run unaffected. Consequently, in the main Timeline of this movie, only one frame is used. Movie clips are useful in situations in which you need to continually loop an animation or, in our case, a situation in which we need to control animations on mouse rollover and rolloffs.

STEP 01

file
SETUP

First, I set the movie dimensions at 80 wide by 60 high via Modify > Movie. I typically set the fps (frames per second or "frame rate") depending on my target playback environment. If I know that the target machine is a 233 or higher and the target modem is 56k and higher, I might push my frame rate up to 20 fps, keeping in mind that a fast frame rate is going to affect streaming, because frames (assets) are being called upon sooner, and that the more frames the heavier the file size. On the other hand, if my file is going out to the general public, I will set the frame rate to 12 fps or lower and will always test on 28.8 with a slow machine to ensure acceptable playback. For this project, I'll set the frame rate at 12 fps.

Also, I set up my Flash layers, from top to bottom, in this order:

labels
action
sound (snd)
dave
film
button
background (bg)

Your layers should resemble those shown in figure 04:01.

As with the previous examples in this book, I insert a rectangle the same size as my stage in the background layer and create a symbol (F8) of it. This allows me to control the color of the background initially and throughout the movie playback. The button layer in this file will hold an invisible button that defines the interactive onscreen area.

figure 04:01

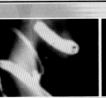

preparing the VIDEO

When I first started designing Flash spots, my illustration skills were somewhat undeveloped. In fact, they were non-existent. I had come from a Photoshop and Director background—both bitmap tools—and rather than sit down and learn how to control a Bézier curve, I decided instead to force my limited skillset on Flash. My lack of ability in the area of vector illustration combined with my love of film and film titles pushed me in a bitmap-driven, cinematic direction with Flash. Although I have since learned to work the vector tip, this cinematic direction remains a huge part of my style. The trick here usually is to shoot video in short spurts and hope you capture something compelling.

For the hillmancurtis.com navigation page, however, I was able to find film edit effects—random film leaders, splices, and grain—on a video source CD-ROM. The film effect clip I use in this file is from a royalty-free video clip collection by Radius and can be found and purchased at http://www.digitalorigin.com/products/filmtextures.html.

How you manage to get the film or video is not as important as how you go about processing it for use in Flash. Having found the video source, my first step was to import it into Adobe Premiere. Premiere is a desktop digital video editing tool used for everything from video production for CD-ROMs to offline editing for broadcast. It's a good all-around digital video editor, and that's why I use it. Again, regardless of your choice of video editing tools, the logic will remain the same. You will export digital video as sequential bitmaps.

You must digitize your video before you can take advantage of this and other video editing programs. Many computers come with a low-quality video digitizer standard. Other options include purchasing a video digitizing card, which ranges from $300 to $5,000, or finding a service bureau that will digitize your footage for you. Finally, if you don't have either a video camera or a digitizing card, you can purchase license-free digital video that comes on a CD-ROM. http://www.photodisc.com is one site that offers such discs, and the hillmancurtis.com site (http://www.hillmancurtis.com/book) has a download area for video as well.

The Premiere 5 work area shares some features with Flash 3. There is a Project window, which acts much as the Library does in Flash. This is where your assets reside, whether imported into or created within Premiere. The Monitor window is much like the "stage" in Flash. This is where you can view your project. And the Timeline is a linear, layer-based Timeline where you can apply your video cuts and effects.

To prepare a digitized video clip in Premiere for use in Flash, follow these steps:

1 Choose File > Import > File, and select the digitized video file.

2 Drag the video from the Project window onto a layer of the Timeline.

The video appears in the Timeline as well as in the monitor window as shown in figure 04:02.

By clicking and dragging the Timeline playhead, you can scrub through my video clip. *Scrubbing* is sort of like manually forwarding or rewinding through the clip.

3 Scrub until you find a small portion of the video to use as the loop.

4 When you find a section of the video you are happy with, set the work area bar to reflect the in and out point of your selection as shown in figure 04:03.

figure 04:02

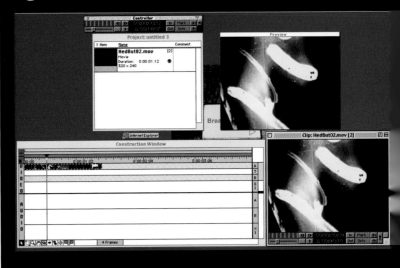

figure 04:03

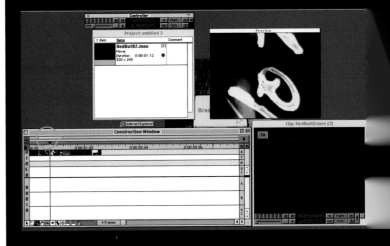

continues

5

Choose File > Export > Movie, and when the Export Movie dialog appears, click on the Settings button.

The Export Settings dialog is where you can set the output file type, audio and video compression, frame rate, movie size, and rendering options. For this example, you need only focus on the file type output, frame rate, and frame size.

6

For file type output select Windows Bitmap Sequence (or Pict Sequence for Macintosh) and choose Work Area as the Range option (see figure 04:04). When you're done, click Next.

7

Enter a frame size in pixels and specify the frame rate.

For my frame size I input 80 by 60, which was the button size I came up with when laying out the design in FreeHand. In the Frame Rate box, I selected 10, which means that I will export 10 individual bitmap frames per second (see figure 04:05).

What you want to do here is choose a frame rate that will give you relatively smooth motion, but will not export too many frames. Think of it this way: Each frame is going to cost you in size in your final Flash movie. You want an immediate download, or as close to an immediate download as you can get, and that translates to the fewer frames the better. Because I had set my work area to cover just under 2 seconds, setting my frame rate at 10 means I'll end up with roughly 18–20 bitmaps. I can work with that.

Now, let's complete the export operation.

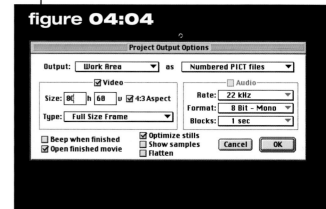

figure 04:04

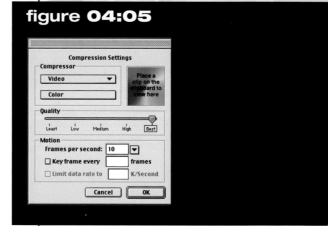

figure 04:05

8

Before exporting, create a folder in which to save the bitmaps. Then, click OK to display the Export Movie dialog and enter a base name for the bitmaps. Click Save to save the files in the folder.

Premiere saves each frame of your digitized video as an individual file, named sequentially. For example, if I choose "filmClip" as my base name, the first three frames would be called filmClip01.bmp, filmClip02.bmp, and filmClip03.bmp.

importing sequential bitmaps into Flash— CREATING MOVIECLIP 1

Now that you've exported your sequential bitmaps, you'll import them into Flash. The folks who designed Flash (Jon, Robert, and team) thought about this and made it easy for us. Read on; you'll see what I mean.

Follow these steps for importing the sequential bitmaps into Flash:

1 In Flash, choose Insert > New Symbol.

2 In the Symbol Properties dialog, enter a name for the symbol such as **filmclip1** and select the Movie Clip option as shown in figure 04:06. Click OK and the Symbol edit environment will open.

3 In the Symbol edit environment, double-click on the first layer in the Timeline and name it **filmloop** or something similar.

figure 04:06

Symbol Properties	
Name: filmclip1	OK
Behavior: ● Movie Clip	Cancel
○ Button	
○ Graphic	Help

continues

4 Create two more layers for labels and actions (see figure 04:07).

These additional layers are going to be important for programming the rollover behavior of the buttons later.

5 Choose File > Import to bring in the sequential bitmaps previously exported from your video editing program—in our case, Premiere.

6 Select the first bitmap of your sequence in the Import dialog and click Open.

If you have a series of bitmaps that are named sequentially (such as film01, film02, and so on), Flash offers to import them sequentially.

7 A dialog appears asking if you'd like to import all of the images of the sequence—click Yes to confirm.

Notice that Flash has imported the bitmaps sequentially over the Timeline with each one in its own keyframe (see figure 04:08). Try playing the sequence by choosing Control > Play or by pressing Enter (Return). Be on the lookout for non-essential bitmaps you can delete. Non-essential bitmaps include bitmaps that resemble one another closely or perhaps are blurred or flawed visually.

figure **04:07**

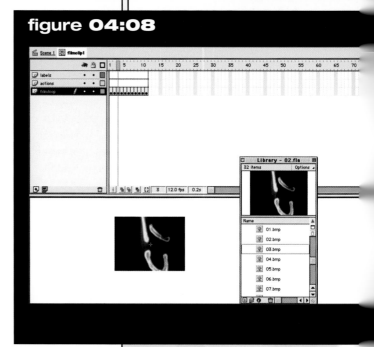

figure **04:08**

8 In the same manner that you scrubbed through the clip in Premiere, scrub through these frames. Click and drag your playhead through each frame, deleting any non-essential bitmaps. To do this quickly, select the keyframe that you want to delete and, while holding down the Shift key, press F6.

Although each project will vary, it's often surprising how few frames are "enough." In many cases, you should be able to eliminate all but seven or eight frames. If a transition between two frames is particularly jarring, try adding a frame between the two keyframes, as shown in figure 04:09.

figure 04:09

STEP 04

aligning the imported
BITMAPS

When you are satisfied with your sequence, center all of the bitmap images using the Edit Multiple Frames feature. This is a super cool feature in Flash…a real time-saver…if you know what I mean.

1 Select the Edit Multiple Frames button located at the bottom of the layers window (see figure 04:10).

continues

2 A work area slider will appear at the top of the layer window. Pull it across all of the frames as shown in figure 04:10.

3 Select all in the Align Panel and center all the bitmaps. Make sure you have Align To Stage selected in the Align Panel.

Importing sequential bitmaps into a symbol means that each bitmap is listed separately in the Library. It's a good idea to use Flash 5's folder capability to place all these images—along with their corresponding movie clips—in a separate folder as described in Chapter 2.

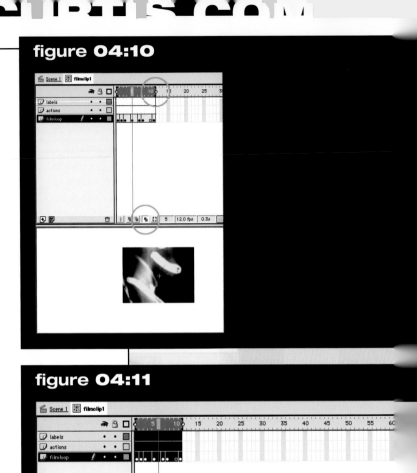

figure **04:10**

figure **04:11**

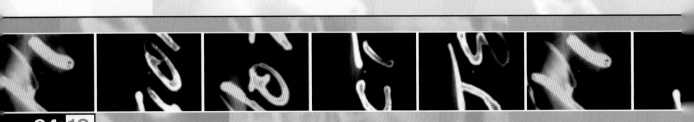

importing sequential bitmaps into Flash— CREATING MOVIECLIP 2

Use the same import process described to create movieclip1 to create your second movieclip. Because the second movie clip will appear when the button is rolled-over by the user's pointer, you'll obviously want to select a noticeably different piece of video. For the hillmancurtis.com navigation buttons I chose a video of an eye opening. For this re-creation, I used a portion of a video I shot with my digital camcorder of a friend, Dave Hartt. I named this symbol "daveclip1" (see figure 04:12).

figure 04:12

Symbol Properties

Name: daveclip1

Behavior: ● Movie Clip
○ Button
○ Graphic

OK
Cancel
Help

scripting the loop action FOR MOVIECLIP1

Each of the video clips by itself lasts no more than a second, if that. For them to always be playing, the clips must loop continuously. In Flash, we can create a loop by using a "go to and play" action that sends the playhead back to the beginning of the sequence when it reaches the end of that sequence. As always, I place this action in the separate layer that I have created and titled "actions."

I also use Flash's label facility as much as possible. Not only does this give me an overall understanding of what's happening when, but it also simplifies the programming process. Rather than refer to a frame number when building an action, I reference a label previously placed in my label layer.

1 Open the editor for the initial movie clip, filmclip1, by double-clicking on it in the symbol library.

2 In the labels layer, double-click the keyframe in frame 1.

continues

3
In the label field of the Frame Panel, enter filmstart or something similar.

Be sure that the Label option is selected; a Flash Comment cannot be used in programming actions (see figure 04:13).

4
Add an extra keyframe (use the keyboard shortcut F7) in all * the layers after the last frame of the sequence (see figure 04:14). In the labels layer, double-click on that blank keyframe, and using the Frame Panel, name the label Filmstop.

The idea here is that when the user rolls over the button, the playhead will be instructed to go to frame label "film stop" and stay there while the movie clip of Dave plays.

5
In the actions layer, insert a keyframe in the second-to-last frame of the movie clip and double-click it to open the Frame Actions Panel.

6
From the Basic Actions list, drag Go To into the script window. The options for the selected action are displayed at the bottom of the window (make sure you have Normal Mode selected by using the keyboard shortcut Ctrl-N / Cmd N).

7
In the Type drop-down, choose Frame Label and select the label representing frame 1, in this case "filmstart."

8
Make sure the Go To and Play option is checked at the bottom of the Frame Actions Panel.

figure **04:13**

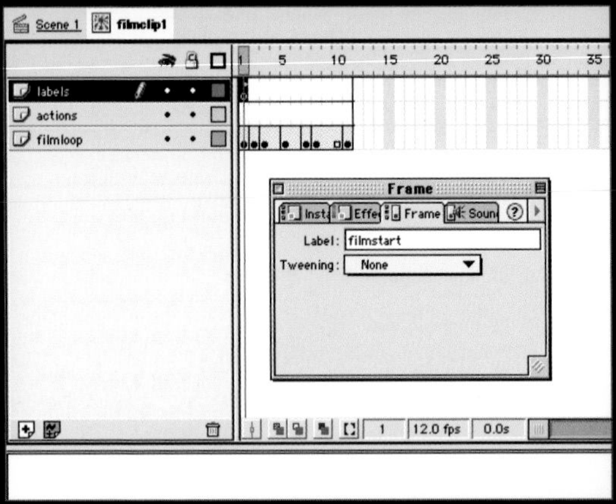

figure **04:14**

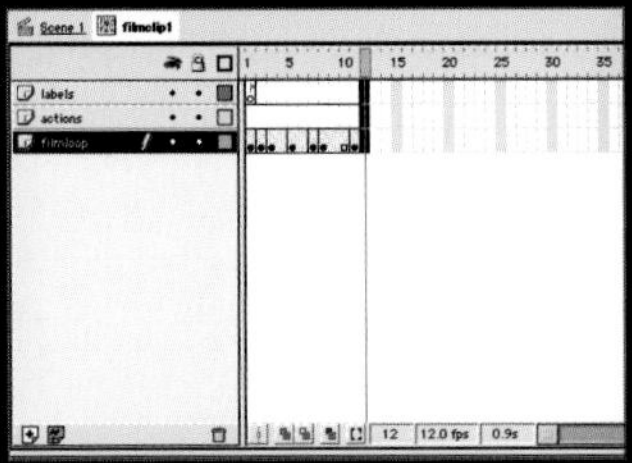

figure **04:15**

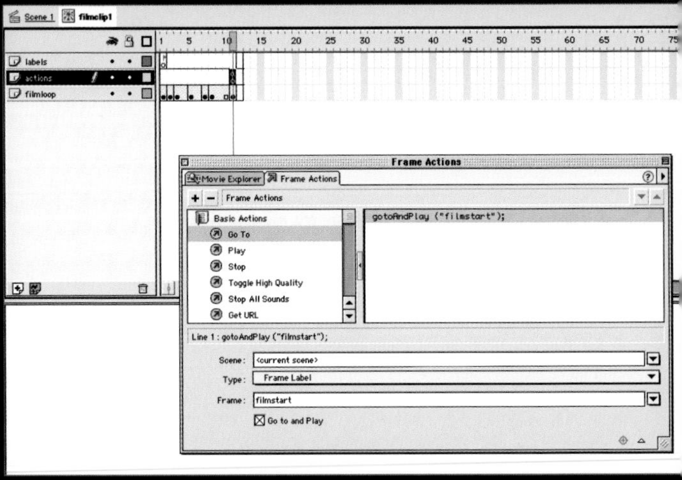

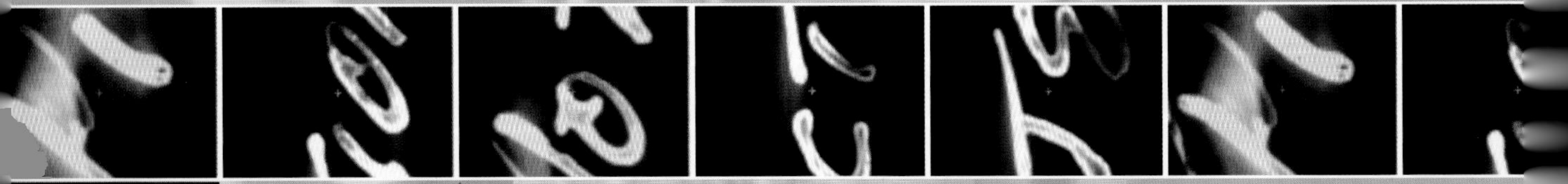

STEP 06

scripting the movie clip
FOR ROLLOFF ACTION

Now that you've created the loop action for one film clip, it's time
to do the same for the second clip. Because this clip will play only
when the user's pointer rolls over the button and then stop when it
rolls off, there are a few variations in the technique.

1 Open the second movie clip
for editing.

2 In all layers, insert a blank
keyframe at frame 1. You should
already have blank keyframes in
the actions and labels layers
since by default flash puts a
blank keyframe in frame one of
any layer. To add the blank
keyframe in the daveloop layer,
select all of the keyframes and
click and drag them, as a unit,
one frame to the right as shown
in figure 04:16.

3 Add a frame (using the keyboard shortcut F5) at the end of
both the labels and actions layers so that all of the labels have
an equal number of frames.

4 In the labels layer, insert a label
in frame 1 named **davestop** or something
similar…since Dave is somewhat of a freak, I guess I
could have called the label freakstop…but let's stick
with davestop.

5 In frame 2 of the label layer, insert a second label
titled **daveloop**.

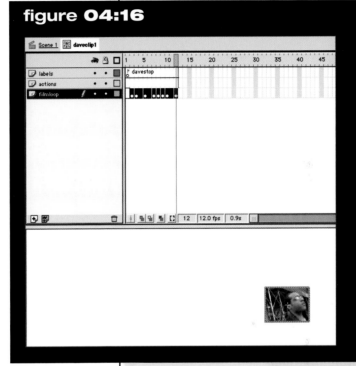

figure **04:16**

continues

6 In the actions layer, double-click the blank keyframe on frame 1 to open the Frame Actions Window.

7 From the Basic Actions list, drag Stop into the script window. This keyframe is used to stop the movie from playing until explicitly activated.

8 On the last frame of the action layer, insert a blank keyframe (using the keyboard shortcut F7), double-click the blank keyframe, and add a Go To action. Set the label target to the daveloop label, making sure to select the Go To and Play option at the bottom of the window, as shown in figure 04:17.

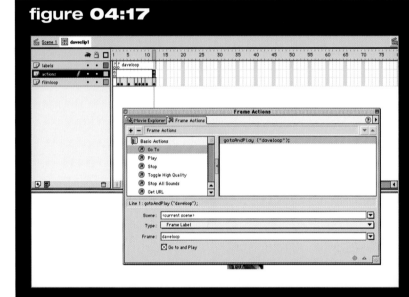

figure 04:17

So here's where we're going with this…filmclip 1 will be looping from the moment the movie loads on the web page, but on the layer right above filmclip1 is daveclip1, invisible because we have stopped daveclip1 on a blank frame (as shown earlier). When the user rolls over, we will tell filmclip1 to go to the label called filmstop, which is all blank frames (filmclip disappears) and at the same time we'll tell daveclip1 to start playing (daveclip appears). So…filmclip1 stops playing…daveclip1 starts. Confused enough yet?…Don't be; stay with me here as we add the button that will command all of this….

adding a
BUTTON AREA

Within Flash, a *button* is a particular type of symbol that includes four—and only four—frames. The first three frames (the Up, Over, and Down states) are separate images that appear according to what the user does. The fourth frame, the Hit state, is invisible and serves to define the interactive area. After the size and shape of the Hit state is set up in the button symbol, an instance of that symbol is inserted into the movie and assigned actions.

To insert a button for interactive use, follow these steps:

1 Create a new symbol called button by choosing Insert > New Symbol.

2 In Symbol Properties dialog, select the Button Behavior option.

When the Symbol Editor opens, you'll notice that four frames have been assigned and labeled. Use the fourth frame of a button to define the interactive, or Hit, area.

3 Select the Hit frame, which is frame 4, and add a blank keyframe (using the keyboard shortcut F7) as shown in figure 04:18.

figure 04:18

4 With the hit keyframe still selected, drag an instance of the bg symbol from the library.

5 Using the Align Panel, center the bg symbol. Be sure to select the Align To Stage option in the Align Panel, to center your symbol within the movie window. This bg symbol will not be visible in your movie; it exists only in the hit frame.

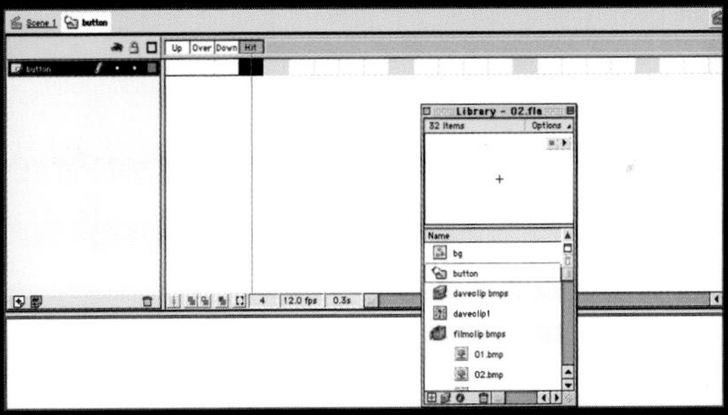

continues

6 Return to the Movie Editor by choosing Edit > Edit Movie (Ctrl-E / Cmd-E).

7 On frame 1 of the button layer, drag an instance of the just-created button from the Library to the stage. In the Align Panel, center the rectangle. Again, be sure to check the Align to Stage option in the Align dialog.

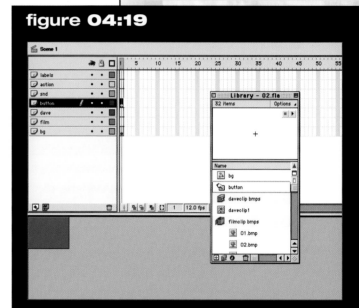

figure 04:19

Notice that the button appears blue (see figure 04:19). This is a feature that allows you to see the invisible button in case you need to move it. If your button does not appear blue, choose Control > Enable Simple Buttons (in this example, you'll want to uncheck the Enable Simple Buttons) or use the keyboard shortcut Ctrl-Alt-B / Cmd-Option-B. This is a toggle that turns on, or activates, your buttons in the Flash editor.

8 To test the button, select Control > Enable Simple Buttons to activate the button.

When Enable Simple Buttons is engaged, a pointed finger icon appears when you move your mouse pointer over the button, just as it would when the movie is viewed in a web browser.

9 When you are finished testing your button, select Control > Enable Simple Buttons again to disable the feature and allow continued editing.

STEP 08

naming movie clip
INSTANCES

Because we're going to issue actions that will control the two different movie clips (stopping one, starting the other), it's essential that you name both instances of the movie clips uniquely. Naming the instances of the movie clips allows Flash actions to be targeted to each specific instance. In other words, when the user rolls over the button, an action will be given both to stop filmclip1 and start playing daveclip1.

1 Select the film layer.

2 From the library, drag to the stage an instance of filmclip1 and center align it using the Align tool.

3 Select the instance of the first movie clip by clicking on the keyframe, which you just placed in the main movie's Timeline.

4 Select the Instance Panel.

5 In the Instance Panel, enter a unique name in the Name text field. Name it filmclip1 as shown in figure 04:20.

6 Repeat steps 1–5 for the second movie clip with the following differences:

- Drag the instance of daveclip1 to the dave layer.

- In the Instance Panel, name this instance **daveclip1**.

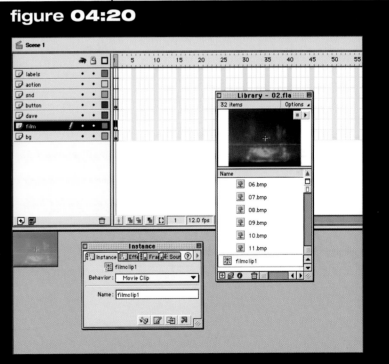

figure 04:20

coding the BUTTON

Now that the movie clips are in place, we need to tell them what to do and when. For a basic rollover, the coding is fairly straight-forward:

- When the user's pointer moves over the hit area, stop playing filmclip1 and begin playing daveclip1.

- When the user's pointer moves off the hit area, stop playing daveclip1 and resume playing filmclip1.

I guess I've stressed the logic of this button enough at this point....

To add the necessary actions for controlling the rollovers, follow these steps:

1 Lock all layers except the button layer by pressing Alt / Option while clicking on the button layer lock control as shown in figure 04:21.

2 Select the button in the button layer and choose Windows > Actions or use the keyboard shortcut Ctrl-Alt-A / Cmd-Option-A.

3 The Objects Actions Panel is displayed.

4 From the Basic Action list, drag the On Mouse Event action into the script window.

The initial code is written into the list window and the On MouseEvent options appear at the bottom of the window. Make sure you have Normal Mode selected (Ctrl-N / Cmd-N).

figure **04:21**

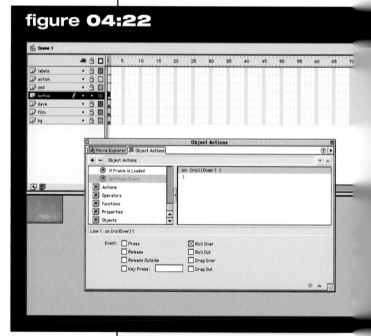

figure **04:22**

5 Select the Roll Over checkbox from the available options and uncheck the Release checkbox (see figure 04:22).

Remember, on rollover, the first thing you want to happen is to stop filmclip1 from playing. To do this, you must first specify that clip as the one you want to control via the Tell Target action.

6 Double-click the Tell Target action in the Basic Actions list. Make sure in the script window you have the first line of code selected. This is the Tell Target action added inside the Roll Over action.

7 Click on the small cross hair at the bottom right of the Actions window to set the target.

From the available list, choose filmclip1. Click OK. The filmclip1 target is added to the code.

After you've found the proper target, it's time to specify the action(s).

8 From the Basic Actions list, double-click Go To. Make sure Go To and Play is unchecked.

The code should now say gotoAndStop.

9 Select Frame Label from the Type drop-down list and type filmstop in the Frame field (see figure 04:24).

The second part of the onMouseOver event is to start the second movie clip

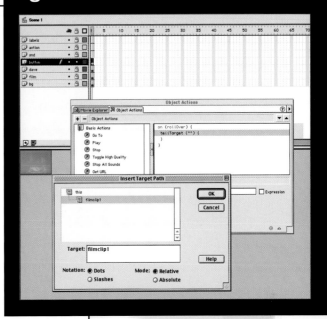

figure 04:23

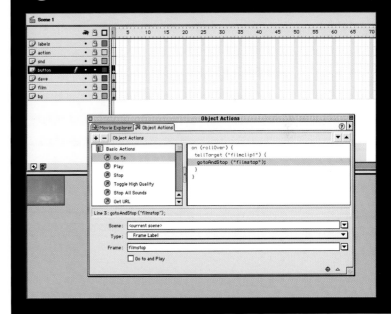

figure 04:24

continues

playing. You insert actions
identical to those just created;
however, the actions have
different parameters.

10 Select the second to last curly
bracket in the script.

This is the end of the Tell Target
action.

11 Repeat steps 6–10, changing the
parameters like this:

- For Tell Target, choose
  daveclip1.

- Rather than the Go To action,
  select the Play action.

The resulting code should look like that
shown in figure 04:25.

figure 04:25

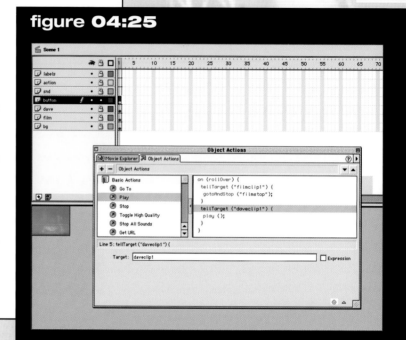

setting the rolloff
BEHAVIOR

You can now close the Instance Properties dialog and test your
code. You can only test movie clips by choosing Control > Test
Movie. Notice that although the rollover works fine, the movie
clips don't revert when your pointer moves away from the button,
as they should. To add the rolloff behavior, follow these steps:

1 Select the button in the button layer.

2 Choose Windows > Actions or use the keyboard
shortcut Ctrl-Alt-A / Cmd-Option-A.

3 In the Object Actions Window, select the last line of
the script (i.e., the last curly bracket).

continues

4 From the Basic Actions list, double-click the OnMouse Event action.

5 Select the Roll Out checkbox from the options at the bottom and deselect the Release checkbox.

6 From the Basic Actions list, double-click the Tell Target action and choose daveclip1.

7 Double-click the Go To action in the Basic Actions list and select the Frame Label option from the Type drop-down list. Enter the label name of the stop frame, in my case "davestop."

8 Select the second to last curly bracket, the end of the Tell Target statement.

9 Repeat steps 6–8, changing the parameters like this:

- For Tell Target, choose filmclip1.

- Select the Play action.

When you're finished, the script should resemble the one shown in figure 04:26.

The final bit of code I include is not necessary for the rollover effect, but is required if I want to use the buttons as navigational devices. Using the same process as described earlier, I add a third On Mouse event: On (Release). This event triggers when a user presses and releases a mouse button. The action taken is Get URL, which opens up a specified web page. The URL can be either absolute (such as http://www.*yourURL*.com/) or relative (as in products/index.html) and you can also specify the window in which you want it to appear. If you'd like to replace the current page, choose the _self window. Also, if you want the button to navigate within your Flash movie you can add a GoTo action on the release mouse event and simply specify the frame number or label you want to go to.

figure 04:26

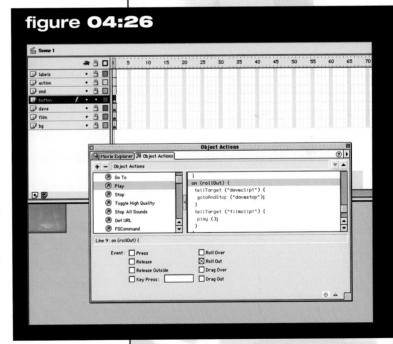

adding Flash text
TO THE MOVIE

It's also possible for you to include Flash text over movie clip rollovers. The button, previously used just to define an interactive area, can also be employed to hold text or another visual element. Naturally, it's up to the artist to decide what aesthetically is appropriate, but the technique is very simple.

To overlay text on the movie video clip, follow these steps:

1 Select the keyframe in the button layer and choose Edit > Edit Symbols.

2 Add keyframes to the frames where you want the text to appear.

If, for example, you want text to appear during a rollover, add a keyframe to frame 2, the Over state.

3 Select the first keyframe where you want to add text.

4 Select the Text tool and add the desired text.

5 If desired, select another keyframe and add additional text.

When you test the movie, your text appears along with your rollover or other programmed effects. As an example, I added the word "over" to frame 2 (the Over state) of my button (see figure 04:27).

figure 04:27

6 Return to the Movie Editor and drag the button layer up two layers so that it is above both the film and dave layers, as shown in figure 4:28.

7 Choose Control > Test Movie. You should see the text "over" upon rollover of the button.

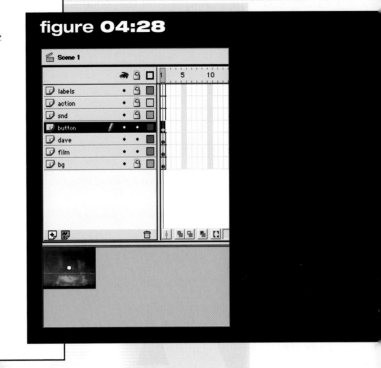

figure **04:28**

conclusion

This is a very cool technique, multi-state animated rollovers. You can really create some awesome buttons and add a deeper interactive experience to your page. Instead of just a button, you can create a navigational element…one that's compelling and adds to the message you wish to communicate on your page. This chapter introduced some serious food for thought. You can see how you can control separate movie clips. Think about that…the sky's the limit. Pretty soon you'll be controlling movie clips that control other clips that return results based on…well I could go on, but you get the point. In this chapter we just scratched the surface of Flash 4 programming. We'll get deeper into it in Chapter 8, "Deconstruction: ManiFestival Site," but kicking out some cool multi-states, justified multi-states…that communicate, can be a big plus for your site.

3D WIREFRAME

05:05:05

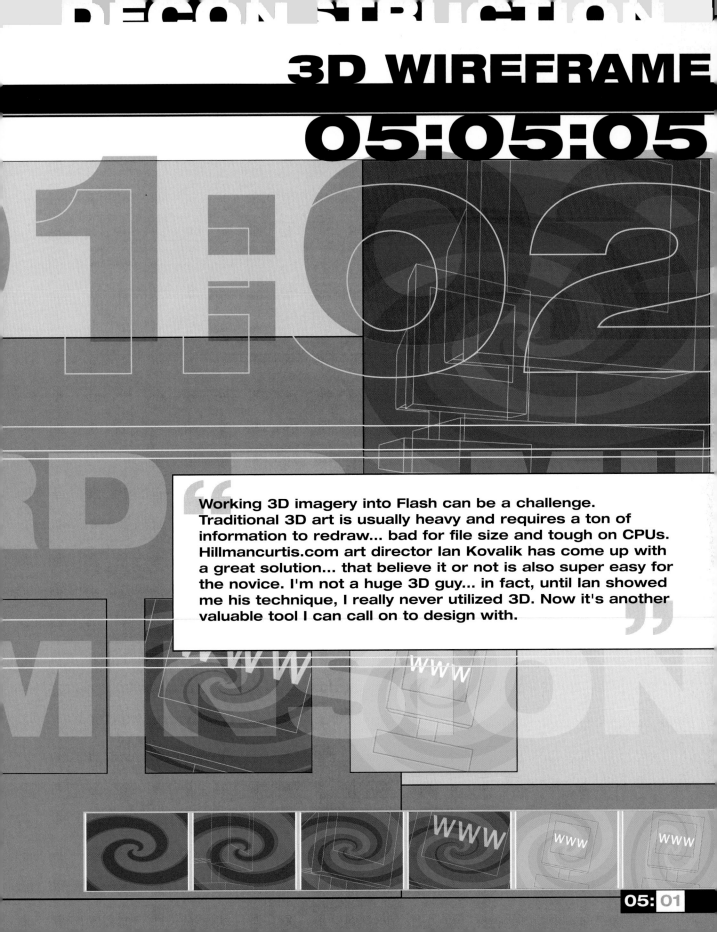

"Working 3D imagery into Flash can be a challenge. Traditional 3D art is usually heavy and requires a ton of information to redraw... bad for file size and tough on CPUs. Hillmancurtis.com art director Ian Kovalik has come up with a great solution... that believe it or not is also super easy for the novice. I'm not a huge 3D guy... in fact, until Ian showed me his technique, I really never utilized 3D. Now it's another valuable tool I can call on to design with."

BEHIND THE DESIGN

Working 3D imagery into Flash can be a challenge. Traditional 3D art is usually heavy and requires a ton of information to redraw—bad for file size and tough on CPUs. Hillmancurtis.com art director Ian Kovalik has come up with a great solution that, believe it or not, is also super easy for the novice. I'm not a huge 3D guy; in fact, until Ian showed me his technique, I really never utilized 3D. Now it's another valuable tool I can call on to design with. That said, I will turn this chapter over to our gifted art director, Ian Kovalik…

In our experience, adding a 3D element to a Flash movie can be entirely rewarding or it can end up wasting a lot of time. Like any production process, it's good to consider whether it's worth devoting time to. Playing my own devil's advocate, I might dare ask, "Why use 3D?" One could presumably accomplish any goal in Flash without ever needing to think in more than two dimensions. Indeed, this book is full of great examples that don't use 3D. So why use it? The answer falls back on our favorite theme of communication: Everything we put into a movie should communicate something—a brand, an idea, or an emotion. And so it goes with 3D.

Looking over our portfolio, I've noticed that almost all the 3D elements we've used relate directly to our movies' focus. In a recent spot for a reputable computer company, the client wanted to give its viewers a sense of the company's history and longevity. To represent this idea, it chose to feature the garage out of which the company was founded. Up to this point, all we had of the famous garage were a couple of static photos. We saw this as the perfect opportunity for 3D, and created a simple 3D version of it (see figure 05:01). With the element in our arsenal, we were able to isolate the garage and move it through space—and at the same time, give it an almost mythic quality. Right from the start, the ad was a big hit—with the client and with the client's viewers—and this was due in part to a judicious use of 3D.

Another industry giant (computers, of course) posed us with a particularly exciting challenge: to build an ad that would demonstrate just how much its processor could expand a user's Internet experi-

ence. The client asked if we could add depth to the ad—literally—and we immediately started sketching out ideas in 3D. In the final product, the main element is a three-dimensional computer. Later on in the chapter, I'll take a version of the element and demonstrate exactly how it was created and brought to life. But first, a word or two about laying down the foundations of the production process….

an overview of OUR PROCESS

Regardless of your level of experience with 3D, it's important to understand the logic behind incorporating a 3D element into a Flash movie. Flash—in its current incarnation—is a 2D authoring environment and is not intended for displaying 3D animations. To take advantage of the unique look of 3D, one must maximize the production metaphor that Flash provides, namely flat, two-dimensional frames.

To make things easier, we break down our production into two general processes. The first is to design a 3D object or element in a way that focuses on refinement and optimization (with minimal geometry for faster processing and quicker download). To do this, you'll need an external 3D modeler such as

figure 05:01

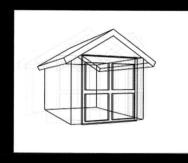

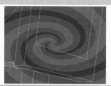

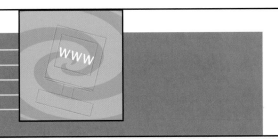

Adobe Dimensions, FormZ by auto.des.sys, or 3D Studio MAX by Kinetix. Once the model is ready, the next step is to import it into Flash, where it is then animated and brought to life.

storyboarding 3D

Planning is essential to keep both the production workload and the final filesize of the 3D movie to a minimum. At the beginning, we like to sketch out any wild idea that may pop into our heads. We're not too concerned with filesize or performance at this point, just a good idea. Once we have that, we can break down the animation into its essential parts and accurately predict whether it's realistic and worth trying. Here are some issues we address at this point in the storyboarding phase:

- **Conceptualizing the 3D object.** "Is it even necessary for the object to be in 3D?" This is a simple but important idea to keep in mind. 3D can add quite a bit to a Flash movie, but is often employed merely as a "wow" factor. Make sure the 3D element has grown out of the overall concept of the piece. Otherwise, it's just icing on the cake (and extra production time).

- **Determining the keyframes.** As in traditional animation, we need to sketch out a storyboard that most clearly describes the motion of an object—in this case, a 3D element. We draw or record only the most extreme instances of the motion, which are referred to as *keyframes*. Practically speaking, this translates into "how the audience is going to view the object." If only the left side will be shown, then there is no need to output images of the opposite side—in fact, there's no reason to build any part of the object that is hidden from view.

Ultimately, the time we save with good storyboarding proves its importance. The more accurate the keyframes, the more time we'll save in the modeling stage of the process.

the 3D modeling PROGRAM

Electing the right 3D modeler helps to keep production time low and manageable. There are a variety of options for both low- and high-end users. For the beginner (or just the impatient) we recommend Adobe Dimensions. Available on the PC and the Mac, Dimensions is a versatile application that is both affordable and easy to learn. Be forewarned, however, that Dimensions isn't the most precise modeler (nor is it meant to be), but it shines when the job calls for a quick text treatment or a simple object render. For these reasons, we chose it to help us demonstrate the first part of our 3D production phase: building the object. Other good modelers include FormZ from auto.des.sys, and 3D Studio MAX from Kinetix. These programs are more intensive and have a greater learning curve than Dimensions, but they offer modeling environments that are far more flexible and precise.

In general, consider these issues when looking into a modeler for 3D Flash production:

- **The simplicity of the modeler.** How quickly can the object be created?

- **The modeler's view options.** How precisely can the user manipulate the camera?

- **The modeler's export options.** Does the modeler export the model in a 2D vector format (typically Adobe Illustrator)?

If you're already experienced with 3D graphics, be sure that your modeler has the capability to export your chosen view of the object in a flat, vector format (usually Adobe Illustrator or Macromedia FreeHand). This feature is crucial to 3D in Flash, and will save you enormous amounts of time over other techniques, such as hand-tracing (decidedly not much of a technique).

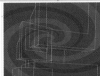

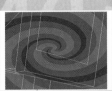

building the object:
THE CPU

Before we can animate anything in Flash, we need an object. The creation of 3D objects can be incredibly involved and complex. It's a challenging discipline and certainly beyond the capacity of this book. To keep things easy and get you up and running, I chose to show a simplified version of our CPU (used in an ad for a popular computer chip maker) and to quickly detail how it could be created in Dimensions.

The simplest way to begin is to think of the object as being made of basic, volumetric shapes—referred to as *primitives*—such as cubes, cylinders, cones, and spheres. With Dimension's Cube tool, we quickly created our object using four rectangular boxes as shown in figure 05:02.

The object at this point is displayed in the axiometric view. This displays an object from the front, side, and top without perspective. Creating an object in a non-perspective view ensures that when perspective is enabled, the object will look correct in all views. Most modelers give you separate modes for the axiometric and perspective views. Dimensions, somewhat confusingly, puts them together in a single control: the Lens option in the Show Camera dialog, found under Window in the main menu. When Lens is set to 0, the object is in the axiometric view. Increasing the value of Lens puts the object into perspective.

figure 05:02

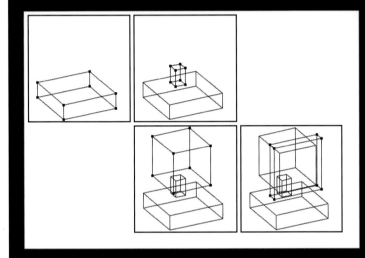

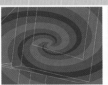

STEP 02

setting the VIEW

Follow these steps to put the object into perspective. This will be the view of the object when it is imported into Flash.

1 Choose Window > Show Camera.

2 Slide up the Lens slider until you have a perspective you're satisfied with—in this example, 94 degrees (see figure 05:03).

figure 05:03

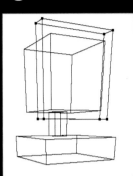

STEP 03

rotating the CPU

I chose this perspective for a particular reason. It will be the last view of the CPU in the final animation, and therefore, the most important. From this keyframe, we'll be able to determine how best to go about producing the rest of the views of the CPU. For this animation, all we need to do is give the object a quarter turn to the left, recording a frame roughly every 10 degrees.

To export the sequence of images, follow these steps:

1 First, select the object or objects you wish to use in the sequence.

continues

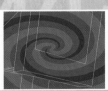

2 Select Operations > Generate Sequence (see figure 05:04). Click OK on the dialog that opens. From this point on, any operation performed on the object will be recorded by Dimensions.

3 Now, rotate the object 90 degrees on the y axis. To do this, use the Rotate dialog, which is found in Operations > Transform > Rotate. Figure 05:05 shows the object rotated at 90 degrees.

This will be the position of the object in the final frame of the sequence. It's also possible to move and scale the object, but not necessary. In fact, it's preferable to wait to perform those manipulations in Flash. This will save filesize, as you'll see later on in the chapter.

4 Select Operations > End Sequence to pull up the Sequence dialog. No more manipulations can be performed on the object at this point. We've found that the maximum rotation one can have in Dimensions is 90 degrees. Entering a number larger than this may yield some unpredictable results. Also, since Dimensions automatically calculates the shortest distance that an object needs to rotate, getting it to perform a full, 360-degree rotation is a little tricky. To do this, you need to generate four separate sequences of rotations—rotating the object 90 degrees with each sequence.

figure **05:04**

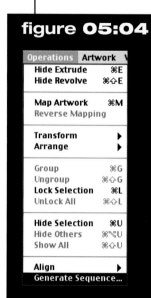

figure **05:05**

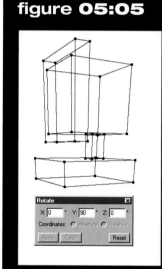

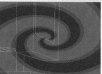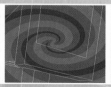

5

In the Sequence dialog, enter the starting frame, enter the number of frames you would like the animation to contain—for this example, we chose Frame10 (see figure 05:06), select Illustrator as the file type, and enter a name for the Filename Prefix. Clicking Generate will call up another dialog asking you to point to a folder. It's a good idea to have an empty folder already set up for the export, since the dialog doesn't give an option to create a new folder.

Dimensions does a very handy thing here. As it exports each file in the sequence, it appends a number to each filename, keeping the sequence in numeric order.

figure 05:06

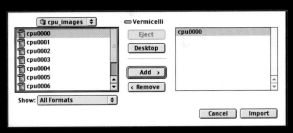

STEP 04

importing the CPU INTO FLASH

The 3D sequence is now ready to be imported into Flash. Once the files are incorporated into a symbol, you can further trim file size by breaking apart the vectors and removing any unneeded segments. To bring a 3D sequence into Flash, follow these steps:

1

In Flash, choose Insert > New Symbol (or use the keyboard shortcut Ctrl-F8) to create a new symbol.

Be sure to give it a meaningful name. Behavior is Graphic. I've called mine cpu_rotate.

2

In the Symbol Editor, select File > Import. Select the first .ai file in the wireframe sequence (see figure 05:07). Flash recognizes the sequence and gives you the option of automatically importing all similarly named files in separate keyframes. Choose Yes to bring in all the sequential files.

figure 05:07

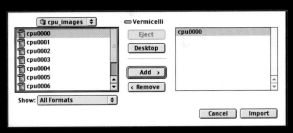

centering the CPU

After the sequence is brought into Flash, you may need to center it relative to the page. To do this, follow these steps:

1 Choose Edit Multiple Frames from the button bar below the Timeline (see figure 05:08).

2 Choose the Modify Onion Markers button (directly to the right of Edit Multiple Frames) and select Onion All from the drop-down menu.

3 Select Edit > Select All (or use the keyboard shortcut Ctrl-A).

4 Click and drag the selected artwork to manually center everything to the page (moving it all together). It's not recommended to use Flash's automatic alignment feature in this case. Using that feature may throw off the object from the center of its rotation and ruin the illusion of 3D motion.

figure 05:08

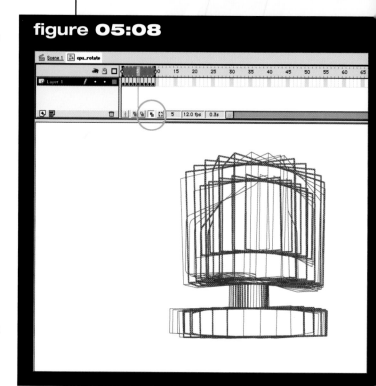

optimizing the CPU

After the 3D object has been imported into the symbol (mine is called cpu_rotate) and centered in the window, it's ready to be optimized. This involves deleting extraneous geometry, which reduces filesize (enormously) and gives the object a look that truly sings.

To do this, start by selecting the artwork in every frame (follow the preceding steps 1–4), then follow these steps:

continues

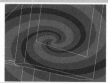

1 Select Modify > Break Apart or use the keyboard shortcut Ctrl-B / Cmd-B). Exercise this once or twice (see figure 05:09):

The object, which was previously grouped, has been broken into a collection of loose, geometric forms (mostly rectangles). These loose forms are free to be dragged away or deleted from the rest of the artwork. Carefully delete the extraneous geometry. This is a quick way to get rid of geometry that might have defined a backface or some other inconsequential element. At this point, it may only be possible to delete a few of the objects (rectangles or triangles), especially if your model was built simply and efficiently.

Figure 05:10 shows what the CPU looks like with some of the geometry removed (and everything has deselected).

2 Next, after choosing Select All again, repeat step 1 until the artwork is completely broken down into line segments (see figure 05:11).

Now, delete any line segment from the artwork that doesn't either define that CPU's shape or fit your intended style. Figure 05:12 shows what I ended up with.

Exercise the previous two simple steps for every frame in the animation. The results are often stunning. This animation, when fully optimized, weighs in at only 2k and plays smoothly with a full ten frames (see figure 05:13).

figure 05:09

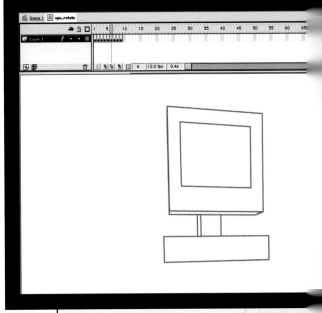

figure 05:10

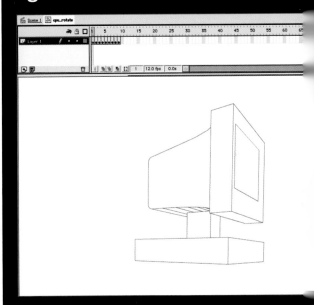

continues

   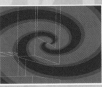 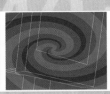 

NOTE

A good tip to use when deleting geometry, especially single lines, is to hold down the Delete key while clicking on the things you want to delete. The offending geometry is zapped away the moment you click.

figure 05:11

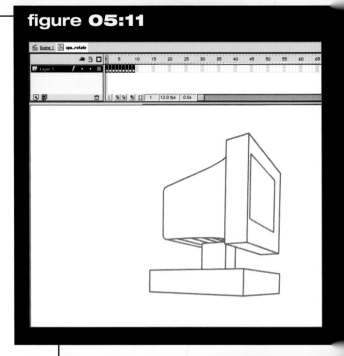

figure 05:12

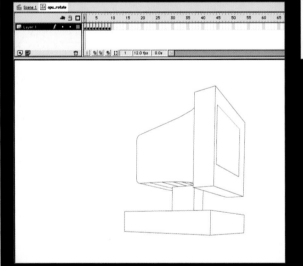

figure 05:13

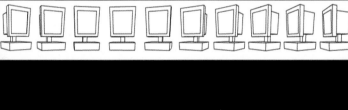

  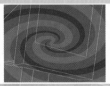 

bringing the object TO LIFE

Now that the CPU has been placed into a symbol and optimized, it's time to be creative. So far, the animation describes only the object's three-dimensional rotation. That's all we ever care to achieve with tools external to Flash. As you're about to see, with Flash's scaling, spinning, Alpha, and color effects, we're about to instill upon the CPU a full range of motion within an unbelievably meager filesize.

The use of Flash symbols is crucial. Our rotating CPU has already been imported into a symbol called cpu_rotate, which we'll be able to reuse, alter, and duplicate without noticeably increasing the size of the file. One technique even capitalizes on the capability of instances to play a single frame rather than the entire symbol.

From this point on, we'll be referring to the actual ad upon which the example CPU (created in Adobe Dimensions) was based. In this spot, we were able to create an opening move that had real impact. Simply rotating the CPU wasn't enough. We wanted to make it seem as if the camera—or the viewer's eye—were moving in space, and we accomplished that with just a few manipulations of the symbol. Follow these steps to see how we did it:

1 Create a layer for cpu_rotate and insert a keyframe on the second frame of the movie.

2 From the Library, drag cpu_rotate onto the stage.

3 Position cpu_rotate so that it is slightly left of center (see figure 05:14).

figure 05:14

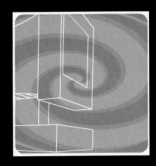

continues

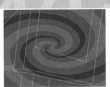

4 Create a keyframe 9 or 10 frames later. Because cpu_rotate is embedded with an animation (of the CPU rotating), the CPU will have animated forward by this frame.

5 With that frame selected, choose Modify > Transform > Scale and Rotate.

6 In the Scale and Rotate dialog, set the Scale setting to 120% and enter **20** degrees in the Rotate field. Click OK when you're ready.

7 Move cpu_rotate to the center of the stage (see figure 05:15).

8 Click somewhere between the first and the second keyframes, then select Insert > Create Motion Tween.

The object should now rotate into view, moving in both two and three dimensions.

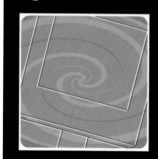

figure 05:15

adding dimension to
THE WIREFRAME

If you look closely at the wireframe CPU in the ad spot, you'll notice that at times it pops out of the screen a bit, like a shaded object. This effect is achieved by adding a second instance of the CPU symbol, slightly offset from the original. By changing the color of the offset instance to all white, the wireframe appears to have depth—all while moving through space.

continues

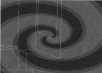

To add dimension to an existing wireframe animation, follow these steps:

1   Create a new layer below the CPU layer and call it **cpu_fx** or something similar.

2   Select all frames of the original 3D object layer as created in Step 7.

3   Drag the selected frames into the new layer while pressing the Alt (Opt) key to duplicate the layer.

4   Select the instance of cpu_rotate in the first keyframe of the cpu_fx layer.

5   Use the arrow keys to move the object one pixel up and one pixel to the left.

6   Select the instance of cpu_rotate in the next keyframe and repeat step 5.

7   Select the instance of cpu_rotate in the first keyframe again.

8   Select the Effect Panel.

9   In the Effect Panel, select Tint from the drop-down list. Set the color to white (255 for Red, Green, and Blue) and the Tint Amount to 100%.

10   Select the instance of cpu_rotate in the second keyframe and repeat step 9.

When you've completed these steps, the wireframe object looks as if it is reflecting light from the upper-left corner of the screen (see figure 05:16).

figure 05:16

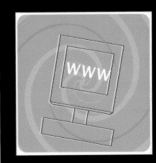

    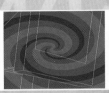 

freezing motion
FOR EFFECT

Right after the opening move, we quickly cut to a slower-paced view of the CPU. This gives the viewer the chance to see the computer in its entirety, and hopefully catch the reference to the Internet (the "www" in the middle of the monitor's screen). At this point in the movie, we've employed a useful production technique that's worth noting: using the Single Frame Play Mode of an instance of a symbol. Remember that the symbol has its own Timeline, which is independent of the main stage's Timeline. All we're doing is freezing the symbol at a point in its Timeline, so we can animate with it as a static object on the main Timeline, which keeps animating. Here's how we made the move, employing the Single Frame Play Mode:

1 In the 3D model layer, place a keyframe where you want the animation segment to begin.

2 Drag out an instance of the 3D model from the Library onto the keyframe.

3 Select the Instance Panel.

4 In the Instance Panel, select Single Frame from the play mode drop-down box, and enter the number of the frame you want to display in the First field. In this case, we chose frame 7 to show the front of the CPU (see figure 05:17).

5 Create a second keyframe 10 frames or so past the first.

6 In the first keyframe (created in step 1), select cpu_rotate and use the Scale tool to reduce it to approximately one-third the size of the stage.

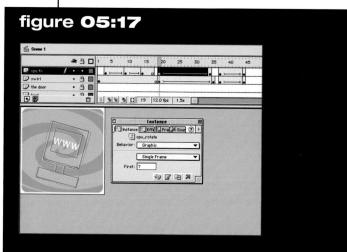

figure **05:17**

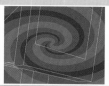

7 In this same keyframe, use the Rotate tool to rotate cpu_rotate +10 degrees.

8 Go to the symbol's second keyframe, scale it two-thirds the size of the stage, and rotate it –10 degrees.

Naturally, the sizes and degrees listed here are just suggestions and are similar to those used in the original spot. The values you choose are dependent upon your movie and design choices.

9 Select the first keyframe again and choose Insert > Create Motion Tween.

When the movie is played, the CPU appears to grow toward the camera while spinning slightly; figure 05:18 shows how this looks against the background used in the Intel Pentium III spot.

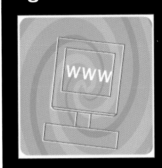

figure **05:18**

STEP 10

motion in PERSPECTIVE

One of our favorite 3D Flash techniques takes advantage of an object's natural perspective to create the illusion of 3D motion. We love this one because it only requires a single frame—unlike a 3D rotation in Flash, which requires several frames.

We employed the technique in the ad for the CPU's final appearance. As shown in figure 05:19, the CPU makes a split-fade and then disappears from view. The ad then moves on to show the client brand and user call-to-action. The split-fade is made from a couple of instances of the same symbol—nothing really new. The twist is that it's done in 3D (see figure 05:19).

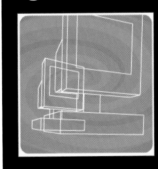

figure **05:19**

continues

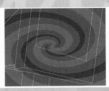

This was accomplished using Flash's scaling feature to animate a single image along lines of perspective. Objects or images that appear to be in 3D often have natural lines of perspective built into them. These lines, also referred to as *orthogonal lines*, point to an artificial horizon line somewhere behind the image (see figure 05:20).

To create the illusion of 3D using an object's built-in perspective, follow these steps:

1 On the main stage, place a keyframe where you want the animation segment to begin.

2 Drag out an instance of the 3D image symbol from the Library onto the keyframe. If the instance is of a symbol containing multiple frames, freeze it on the frame you want to work with using the Instance Panel and Single Frame play mode (as in the previous example).

3 Select the instance in the keyframe and use the Scale tool to reduce the size of the object to about one-fifth the original size, or so. Exactly how much is up to you. Move it to the left a couple of clicks using Shift-left arrow key.

4 Add another keyframe about 10 frames or so after the first.

5 Select the instance in the keyframe and use the Scale tool to increase it to 10 or 15 times the original size. Figure 05:21 shows what your stage might look like with both frames visible.

6 Choose the Modify Onion Markers button (directly to the right of Edit Multiple Frames) and select Onion All from the drop-down menu. Now, toggle on the Onion Skin button. Make sure the layer is unlocked, or the onion skinning will not be visible.

Clearly, the CPU in this case will not animate along the correct lines of perspective (the top and bottom edges of the CPU's sides do not match up). See figure 05:22.

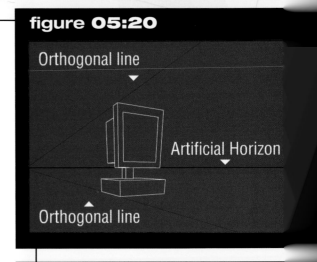

figure 05:20

Orthogonal line

Artificial Horizon

Orthogonal line

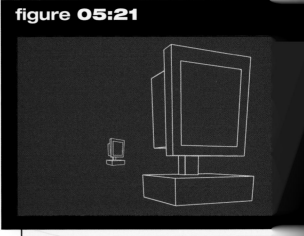

figure 05:21

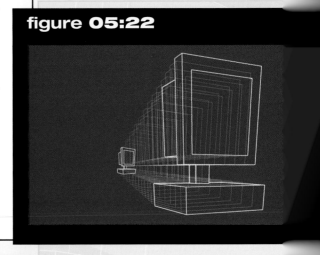

figure 05:22

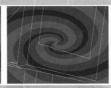

7 To identify correct perspective, select the smaller CPU in the earlier keyframe. Now, using the ghosts of the onion skinning as a guide (and the arrow keys), move the smaller CPU to the left until the top and bottom edges of both CPUs are aligned (see figure 05:23).

In figure 05:23, we've drawn in the lines of perspective for emphasis. When you tween the two keyframes, the result will be a CPU that animates perfectly along the correct lines of perspective using only a single image.

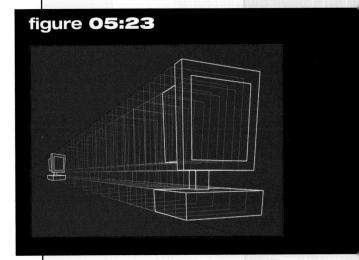

figure 05:23

conclusion

We've introduced and described our two major production phases for 3D Flash—the modeling and the animation—with emphasis on the need for solid planning and efficient execution. We've covered a basic model export (from Adobe Dimensions), given strategies for keeping the 3D models simple and lightweight, covered several key optimization techniques, and demonstrated a number of successful ways to animate 3D in Flash.

With these techniques, you'll now be able to apply exciting 3D elements to your designs—inexpensively and with little effort.

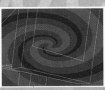

SIX CHAPTER

Sound.

Have their stories told here.

With vide

KLEIN

With video.

With video.

"I try to find the most compelling motion—an interesting swagger or perhaps a dramatic leap—that I can use and reuse on the stage in Flash. In effect, I'm creating digital puppets that can be used later in a Flash movie to illustrate a specific action."

Sound.   Sound.   Sound.   Sound.   Sound.   Sound.

BEHIND THE DESIGN

One alternative to pure-bitmap video is "vectorized" video. Vectorized video is a process where one takes traditional video and converts it to vector-based graphics. With this technique, the Flash designer now has the ability to incorporate extra-ordinarily fluid animations without overloading the movie's overall file size.

Our process utilizes standard multimedia tools, including Flash, to convert video imagery into 2D vectors. In a project for the "FeedRoom" (www.feedroom.com), we took 21 separate vector videos and combined them with traditional video, music, sound, and Flash effects to create a 30-second spot in less than 180k (half of which is audio).

DESIGN FOCUS

Capturing motion
"Vectorizing" video
Tracing bitmaps
Working with "digital puppets"
Reusing symbols to create reverse movement

STEP 01

pre-production
PLANNING

Pre-production planning for creating vector videos is more than a time-saver: It's essential. Several pre-production tips come into play:

- Storyboarding helps you stick to the message and reduces the amount of work at each phase of creation.

- Location scouting and/or set design help to make the background as neutral as possible. For the FeedRoom spot, much of the action was shot against plain white backgrounds or outside on a gray sidewalk under bright sunny skies.

- Costuming is used to distinguish the actors from the setting with solid colors that contrast sharply with the background. Actors in the FeedRoom ad were dressed in black, which further served to reduce the number of post-production steps.

- Lighting is key for cleanly delineating foreground from background and, just as importantly, eliminating or minimizing shadows.

The goal is to capture moving shapes, not images. To reduce your workload, keep that goal in mind every step of the way.

Have their stories told here.

  Have their stories told here.   With video. With video. With video.

 Have their stories told here.

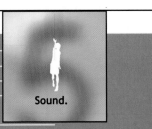

Sound.

STEP 02

motion capture and BITMAP REDUCTION

Video at hillmancurtis.com is generally shot with a digital camcorder and then transferred over a Firewire connection to a video capture card. Once the video is stored on the computer, I'll use an appropriate tool to process it. Either Premiere or AfterEffects—both from Adobe— works well for turning video into vector. Use whatever software you prefer…just make sure it is capable of outputting sequential bitmaps.

After importing the movie into Premiere or any other tool, scrub through the clip until you find the frames containing the motion you want, as discussed earlier and in detail in Chapter 4, "Hillmancurtis.com Navigation." I try to find the most compelling motion—an interesting swagger or perhaps a dramatic leap—that I can use and reuse on the stage in Flash. In effect, I'm creating digital puppets that can be used later in a Flash movie to illustrate a specific action.

Although you can't maintain a full 30 frames per second as with traditional video, you can use a higher number of vector video frames than you could if you were exporting bitmap video frames. For that reason, I tend to isolate a longer sequence of video, really focusing in on a compelling and expressive motion.

The next phase of pre-Flash production is to reduce the number of colors in the video. Doing so saves me a lot of trouble later on, when I'm processing the images in Flash.

To reduce the number of colors, all I need to do is apply a couple of standard filters in Premiere. First, I reduce the video to black and white. Then, I apply levels and manipulate the image to a high contrast.

continues

Sound.

Sound.

Have their stories told here.

With video.

Here's how to do it:

1 Open a new project in Premiere, import a video clip, and drag it to the Timeline. (See the section "Preparing the Video" in Chapter 4, "Hillmancurtis.com Navigation," for details.)

2 After setting the work area bar to reflect the in and out points of your selection, use the selection tool to marquee the clip on the Timeline.

3 With the video clip selected, choose Clip > Filters (or use the keyboard shortcut Ctrl-F / Cmd-F). This opens the Filters dialog.

4 From the list of Available Filters on the left, double-click Black & White. This adds it to the right side of the dialog. You can also select Black & White and then click Add.

5 Now, double-click Levels.

Use the Levels filter in the software to reduce the number of colors in your video before bringing it into Flash.

6 In the Levels dialog, locate the white triangular slider on the Input Levels slider and drag it to the left to increase the brightness of the image. Then drag the gray triangular slider to the right to up the contrast (see figure 06:01).

Obviously, no one setting is right for all videos, so this step takes a fair degree of experimentation. Feel free to try seemingly outlandish choices: You can always go back to your source material.

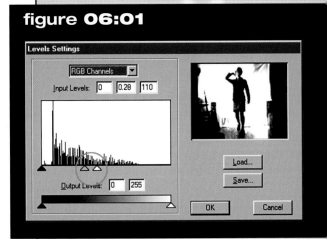

figure **06:01**

Have their stories told here.

With video.   With video.   With video.

7 When you're satisfied with how you applied the filters, click OK. A bright blue bar above the preview video clip in the Timeline will indicate that filters have been applied.

8 Choose File > Export > Movie, and when the Export Movie dialog appears, click on the Settings button and enter the settings. You'll be exporting as Bitmap images (again, see "Preparing the Video" in Chapter 4 for details). Remember, Premiere automatically labels the bitmaps numerically upon export.

STEP 03

video to vectors: converting a bitmap to a vector GRAPHIC IN FLASH

Flash includes a key feature that makes converting video into vectors possible: Trace Bitmap. This tool turns a bitmap image into a vector graphic with discrete areas of color that are editable. It's great for creating stylized illustrations with a posterized look. More importantly, it can save you a tremendous amount of file size when used correctly.

An animation made of bitmaps can be quite heavy, even with a good amount of jpg compression applied. Converting the bitmaps to vectors gives you a smaller overall file and the chance to add more frames to the animation, resulting in a more fluid motion.

continues

Sound.

Sound.

Have their stories told here.

With video.

To convert a series of bitmap video images into vectors, follow these steps.

1 Open a new movie in Flash (use the keyboard shortcut Ctrl-N / Cmd-N).

2 Create a new symbol (use the keyboard shortcut Ctrl-F8 / Cmd-F8) and label it **actionThrow** or something similar, then choose "graphic." This symbol will hold the frames of your "virtual puppet."

3 In the Symbol Editor, choose File > Import (or use the keyboard shortcut Ctrl-R / Cmd-R) and select the first of the sequentially named files that you just created from your video editor. When prompted, confirm that you would like all the files imported as a sequence.

4 Select the bitmap in the first keyframe and choose Modify > Trace Bitmap.

5 Modify the Trace Bitmap settings to get the clearest vector image.

I've set the Color Threshold to 100 (see figure 06:02). The Color Threshold helps Flash determine how to "replace" the bitmap image's pixels with vector shapes. It does this by comparing the color—by the RGB values—of each pixel. If the difference of the RGB values between pixels is less than the Color Threshold value you've entered, then Flash will consider the two to be the same color. The rule to remember is this: The higher the Color Threshold, the fewer the number of colors in the resulting image.

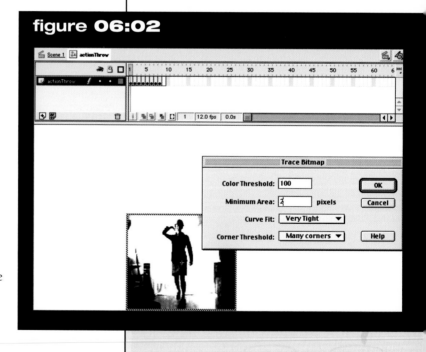

figure 06:02

Have their stories told here.

With video.

With video.

With video.

Have their stories told here.

Modifying the other options within Trace Bitmap (Minimum Area, Curve Fit, and Corner Threshold) also greatly affects the resulting image. Because the possibilities are limitless and depend on the bitmap that you're tracing, I recommend starting with Color Threshold and then going from there. A couple of options, such as Pixels within Curve Fit and Many Corners within Corner Threshold, are generally not recommended and should be tested for file size before being included in your movie (the results often defeat the purpose of the whole Trace Bitmap process—to keep file size down).

6 Set the Minimum Area to a low number as well (see figure 06:03); the example bitmaps were traced with a Minimum Area of 2 pixels. Changing the Minimum Area sets the size of the pixel block that Flash looks at when tracing. The lower the number, the finer the trace.

7 From the Curve Fit drop-down list, select the Very Tight option.

This choice gives you a more detailed vector shape than Normal, Smooth, or Very Smooth. The Pixel option is, in most cases, overkill and ends up giving you a very heavy vector graphic (in terms of file size).

figure 06:03

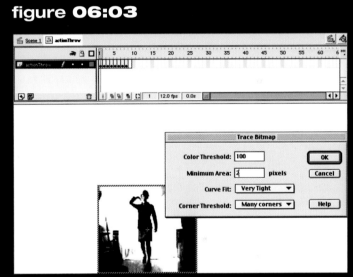

continues

Sound.

Sound.

Have their stories told here.

With video.

8

In the Corner Threshold drop-down list, select Many Corners. Again, this is a good choice when you want a vector shape with detail.

After you've clicked OK to confirm your choices, Flash displays a progress bar as it traces the bitmap.

9

When the tracing is finished, deselect the image. Figure 06:04 shows the image after it has been deselected.

Now, we'll begin eliminating the unnecessary portions of the vector graphic. At this stage, the wisdom of preplanning will become abundantly clear. When a foreground image contrasts sharply with the background, it's much easier to isolate the foreground.

Initially, you'll use the Pointer tool to draw a marquee around large sections of the image you don't want and delete them as shown in figure 06:05.

10

Use the Pointer tool to drag a rectangle around unwanted sections of the traced bitmap.

11

After you've removed the large, unwanted sections of the traced bitmap, use the Zoom tool to magnify areas close to the foreground figure and select other objects to delete.

Be sure to select the background area behind the foreground object, especially if it is white. It's likely that there is another unwanted vector object there. To check for unwanted objects, go into Outline Mode for that layer (the third option located to the right of the layer name). When you're finished, the figure should be clearly delineated.

figure 06:04

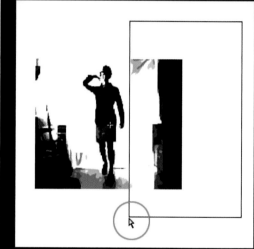

figure 06:05

Have their stories told here.

With video.

With video.

With video.

Have their stories told here.

NOTE

Depending on the video imagery, you may be able to use an alternative technique to clean up each frame. Rather than selecting and deleting those objects you don't want, select all those that you *do* want. Choose Edit > Cut (or use the keyboard shortcut Ctrl-X / Cmd-X). Choose Edit > Select All (or use the keyboard shortcut Ctrl-A / Cmd-A) and delete everything selected. Then, choose Edit > Paste in Place (or use the keyboard shortcut Ctrl-Shift-V / Cmd-Shift-V). This replaces what was cut from the page (what you wanted to keep) and puts it back exactly where it was. Now, your vector graphic is clearly defined on the stage (figure 06:06 shows the graphic enlarged for detail).

figure 06:06

figure 06:07

12 The graphic looks clean, but it is still made of many individual vector objects. Now, you need to consolidate them into one object by using Select All and adding a fill—in this case, black (see figure 06:07). Flash automatically merges the filled objects into a single one. Deselect the graphic.

13 Select the graphic once more and smooth it out with the Smooth tool (see figure 06:08). This refines the image a bit further and saves on file size (the Smooth tool reduces the number of points that define the shape of a graphic—effectively "smoothing it out"; by doing so, the computer has less to keep track of and process).

continues

Sound.

Sound.

Have their stories told here.

With video.

14 Select the next keyframe and repeat steps 5–13 until all keyframes are converted and optimized.

figure 06:08

activating your
VECTOR VIDEO

The vectorized video animation (from the previous section) was used in less than 10 frames of the final FeedRoom spot (see figure 06:09). Although that may seem like a lot of effort for little payoff, working with such detailed animations adds a richness to the work that is otherwise difficult (or impossible) to achieve within a tight file size restriction. The FeedRoom spot is composed of more than 20 single animations—some used repeatedly as recurring design elements. The added bonus, of course, is that each of the vectorized videos is created as a Flash symbol, so there's no file size penalty for reusing elements.

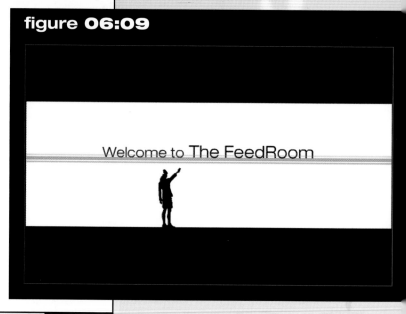

figure 06:09

Welcome to The FeedRoom

continues

Have their stories told here.

With video.

With video.

With video.

The symbol of the "throwing-action" was used in different ways in the FeedRoom piece:

- The sequence is first played straight through—to show the motion.

- The image freezes on the final keyframe of the animation, turns from black to white and scrolls down, off the screen.

To reproduce these effects, follow these steps:

1 In a layer reserved for vectorized videos, place a keyframe.

2 Drag an instance of the symbol from the Library onto the stage.

3 Select the Scale tool to resize the object so that it is approximately half the original size.

4 Position the object near the center of the screen as shown in figure 06:10.

The vector video object is like a puppet that you can place on your stage among other elements. After the motion plays completely, the final frame is frozen and inverted, positive to negative.

5 Create another keyframe on the final frame of the initial motion.

6 Select the Instance Panel. If the panel is not visible, use the keyboard shortcut Ctrl-I / Cmd-I.

figure 06:10

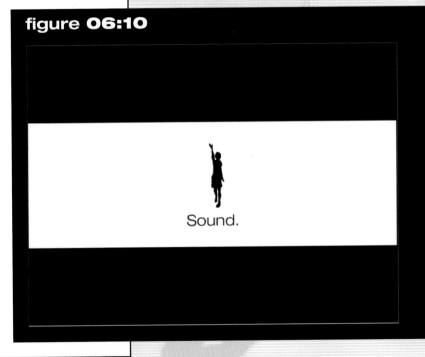

Sound.

continues

Sound.

Sound.

Have their stories told here.

With video.

7 In the Instance Panel, select the Single Frame option using the play mode drop-down list, and enter the number of the frame matching the final frame of the video.

8 Select the Effect Panel.

9 From the drop-down list, choose Brightness and set the slider to 100% so that the figure becomes white as shown in figure 06:11.

After the motion is completed, the vector video holds one position, inverts color from black to white and moves off-screen.

10 Place another keyframe five frames later and reposition the object so that it is almost off the bottom of the screen.

11 Choose the keyframe where the figure turns white and select Insert > Create Motion Tween.

12 Add a blank keyframe after the sequence to end the segment.

figure 06:11

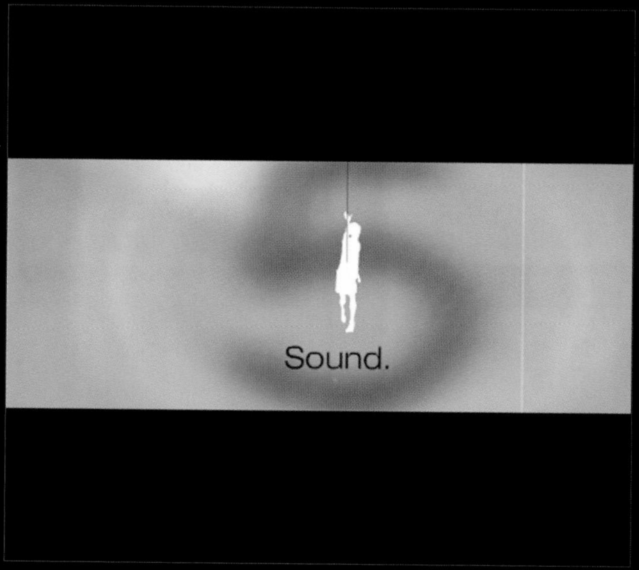

Other Flash techniques included the vector videos used throughout the FeedRoom spot:

- The initial image of the spot has a figure climbing up from the bottom of the stage, seemingly opening a trap door. Here, the positioning of the figure is key to accomplishing the illusion that the figure is emerging from the bottom of the screen.

continues

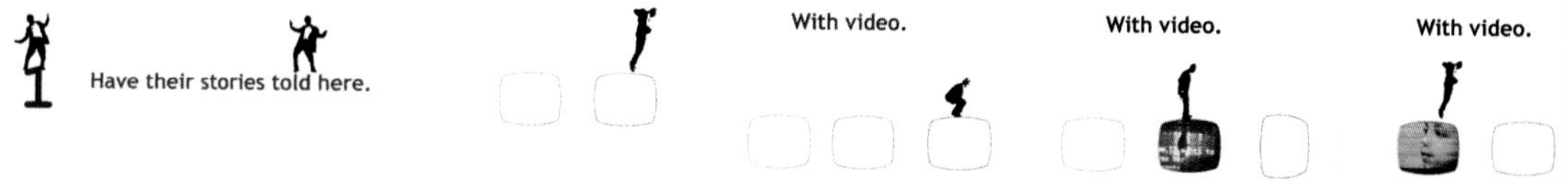

Have their stories told here.

With video.

With video.

With video.

Have their stories told here.

- A figure walks toward the viewer. A simple motion tween where the image is rescaled slightly larger is used to achieve this effect.

- A man struggles to maintain his balance on a stream of 1s and 0s that flow across the screen. The figure was shot pretending to surf; the characters and movement are pure Flash.

- The same man jumps and travels through several screens of information, only to land on a round-cornered rectangle, which fills with video. The jump is frozen on a single frame while the additional information scrolls by. Traditional squash and stretch animation techniques were used to make the landing more real.

creating reverse MOVEMENT

The FeedRoom spot was designed for broadband viewers—still to ensure a steady stream, a looping animation is run while images and audio preload. In the loading sequence, a woman appears to walk in from the left while carrying a "Loading" sign above her head. She reaches center, holds for a moment and then walks off backward to the right. This animation, if it were to stand alone in its own movie, would consist of 32 frames of fluid motion—yet, it would only weigh 14k! The trick is that the animation—which is 32 frames—is really only made of 14 unique vector graphics. If you look closely, the figure's motion is mirrored from left to right. The second half of her walk is exactly the same as the first half—only it's in reverse.

Figure 06:12 shows an abbreviated version of the animation. The frames following the center frame (only three are depicted here) are simply a reverse of the first frames.

figure 06:12

continues

Sound.

Sound.

Have their stories told here.

With video.

This animation could have been shot straight through, but there was really no reason for that. Reversing movement gives the same results, and is quite easy and very economical (from a file-size perspective). Flash 5 can be scripted to play in reverse, but this isn't our only option. For a quick solution that involves zero scripting, follow these steps:

1 Create the vectorized video in the Symbol Editor as described in the earlier section "Video to Vectors: Converting a Bitmap to a Vector Graphic in Flash."

2 After the final keyframe of the original movement, insert several frames to hold the central image: the Loading sign.

3 Create another keyframe after the action is completed.

4 Choose Modify > Instance to open the Instance Properties dialog.

5 In the Definition tab, enter the second-to-last frame number of the sequence in the First Frame field.

For example, for the FeedRoom spot, the loading vector video is 13 frames long; in the First Frame field for the initial reverse keyframe, I would enter 12.

6 Create another keyframe and repeat steps 4 and 5, decreasing the frame count by one.

7 Repeat step 6 until you reach frame number 1 in the First Frame field.

Sound.

Have their stories told here.

Have their stories told here.

With video.   With video.   With video.

06:14

Have their stories told here.

conclusion

The advantages that vectorized video brings to the discipline of web motion graphics is extremely appealing. More than just stylized images, vectorized video makes it possible to create realistic motion that is fluid and expressive. In the FeedRoom spot, we were able to lend an air of playfullness and lightness that wouldn't have come across as strongly with bitmaps or traditional video. Even cooler was the fact that we got all of that motion—character, really—without a huge file size.

With video.

With video.

Sound.

Sound.

Have their stories told here.

With video.

poem by christina n

CHRISTINA MANNING POEM

07:07:07

> " How does one present a midsized poem over the web in a way that would be both functional (no preload) and compelling? I knew I didn't want to have just pretty pictures and scrolling text. In fact, I began to look at this spot as an opportunity to free myself from my reliance on type in motion. "

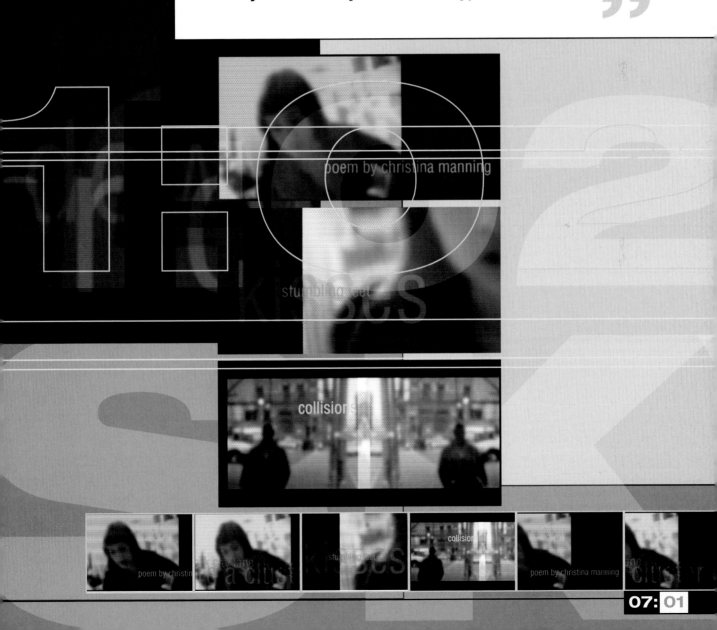

BEHIND THE DESIGN

DESIGN FOCUS

Streaming MP3 audio
Processing audio prior to import
Sharing the stream
One-stop source capture
Optimizing and testing the file

I had been running hillmancurtis.com for almost a year when Gabe Kean, from www.bornmag.com, an online art and literature site, approached me with the offer to design a spot for the NYC-based poet Christina Manning. In the year of running my shop, I had, along with my team, focused almost exclusively on corporate clients—establishing brand and messaging, reinforcing logo recognition, and concepting storyboards and ad treatments. We had worked hard to establish our small team as a leader in targeted rich media and motion graphics and we were buzzed by the work we were doing. Still, when the offer came from Gabe, I jumped at the opportunity. It would give me the chance to work with a ton of freedom and with a poet.

The job presented a couple of challenges immediately; the first was time—I only had a few days I could spare—and the other was more of a design challenge. How does one present a midsized poem over the web in a way that would be both functional (no preload) and compelling? I knew I didn't want to have just pretty pictures and scrolling text. In fact, I began to look at this spot as an opportunity to free myself from my reliance on type in motion.

The solution revealed itself the moment I heard Christina read the poem. Although I was familiar with the poem, I asked her to read it out loud. I wanted to hear the rhythm in the poem. Being aware that poetry is based in cadence and rhythm just as is motion graphics, my thoughts ran to the obvious solution of capturing and reflecting the rhythm of the poem in my spot. But what was more clearly revealed as I listened was that I had no choice but to try and present the poet reading the poem. Her reading style is amazing. I had to use it.

Once I decided to design the spot around Christina's voice-over, I simply broke out my video camera and filmed Christina reading the poem. I figured that with my camera I could capture both the audio and make use of some of the visuals I would later grab from the video. This ended up working great. The challenge then was to come up with a design that used a limited number of bitmaps, reusing those

bitmaps throughout the file to keep the stream free for the audio. Think of it this way…regardless of your viewer's connection, be it a T1 or 56.6 modem, there is a pipeline through which bits of your file stream. If you can come up with a file with assets light enough not to clog the stream, you win. In this case, I carefully chose a total of seven bitmaps pulled from my video of Christina reading that I could reuse throughout the file. I furthered my chances at an open pipeline by blurring the bitmaps in Photoshop prior to importing them into Flash. The blur allowed me the freedom to apply a heavy amount of JPEG compression in Flash without a lot of image breakup.

So, in essence, I targeted the poet's voice-over reading of the poem as the most important element in this file, and then I did everything I could to design around that…carefully constructing a montage of images that relied on repetition, varied scale and angles, overlays, and positioning to keep the spot visually compelling.

All the while, I kept in mind that her voice-over audio stream would be occupying most of my pipeline.

streaming MP3 voiceovers with Flash movies

With long movies, it's difficult to precisely sync audio and video in Flash. Given the high number of variables involved—the wide range of browsers, the huge array of processors and system configurations, and the vagaries of Internet speed and congestion—you might be tempted to throw in the towel. With the introduction of streaming MP3 audio, Flash 5 offers a viable approach to presenting audio over the web.

CHRISTINA MANNING

Sky

Swaying down this dark city lane,
we are a cluster of hands and scarves,
kisses and stumbling feet.
But are these collisions the work of planets
atomic, celestial, or something more earthbound:
walking with you on Broome Street,
catching my heel on a cobblestone, a little drunk.

If matrimony is an astronomy,
inscrutable physics, seen from a distance
(it's true your face in repose
has its familiar constellations,
Venusian lips, your eyes, a quiet firmament),

then I want to understand the valence and force
that holds me to you.
Give me a theorem to live by.
If love is just science
then show me its place in the sky.

MP3 has several clear-cut advantages:

- **Streaming capability.** For audio clips of any length, streaming is a far better alternative than traditional download-and-play. A great deal of web traffic is still traveling on limited dial-up connections with, at best, a 56K modem. Streaming audio allows even these relatively low-bandwidth connections to experience multimedia without the wait.

- **Smaller files size than other codecs.** MP3 compression is state of the art, and the results are wonderfully compact.

- **Superior sound compression.** Streaming ability and small file sizes are solid features but would be worthless if MP3 quality were unacceptable. Fortunately, MP3 files maintain much of the original fidelity for most types of audio including music and, as shown in this demonstration, voiceovers.

Because Flash 4 and Flash 5 are capable of encoding MP3 natively, no special plug-in other than the Flash 4 or 5 player is required. Browsers with the Flash 3 player installed will still be able to view the file—they just won't be able to hear it. This is both good and bad news: On the positive side, if you're authoring a work that is not reliant on audio, then the much larger (at the time of this writing) installed base of Flash 3 users will be able to view it. On the other hand, if the audio is vital to the movie, you have to make sure your audience is aware of the necessity of the Flash 4 or 5 plug-in. (Check out www.moock.org for a free downloadable Javaless Flash player tester. This will tell your viewers which version player they have and instruct them to upgrade.)

recording and processing sound

As with other Flash movies that involve imported media, the first steps with a voiceover are capturing and processing the audio. With today's desktop systems, you can record directly into a program such as SoundForge or SoundEdit 16. The requirements for recording a live performance, as was done in the case of this chapter's example, are very straightforward:

- Secure a microphone with either a mini-jack plug or a mini-jack adapter.

- Ensure that your recording levels are good. In both SoundEdit and SoundForge, there are recording level meters. If the recording volume is too high, the sound will distort; if the volume is too low, the sound won't be properly heard.

- Record in a quiet room. Except in a professional sound studio, it's very difficult to remove ambient noise without affecting the primary sound.

- Capture your audio at the highest sample rate possible. I typically shoot for 44k / 16-bit stereo. Remember that the better the source the better the export.

- Have available plenty of clean hard disk space. Converting any analog signal to digital—whether it's audio or video—is file-intensive. The higher the quality and the longer the audio clip, the larger the file size.

firewire video capture

Most multimedia systems sold today allow you to record audio directly to the hard drive with a microphone. Although I could have used a microphone for the *Sky* piece, I opted to record the artist with my digital video camera (Sony TRV9…about $1,300, although cheaper models can be found—just make sure they have Firewire ports) plugged into the Firewire port.

Let's talk about Firewire. I have to recommend it for video capture. It allows you to capture clean full-screen video on your desktop, with relatively small file sizes. The quality is much better than comparably priced JPEG capture cards, and the playback (you actually view playback on your camera, which remains connected to your computer) is in real time.

All Mac G3s and G4s come with Firewire capture cards stock; for PCs, the cards usually sell for under $500, and for that price they are usually bundled with a full copy of Adobe Premiere. I shop at www.videoguys.com and have been satisfied with their service. So if you are thinking of working video into your Flash work, check out Firewire. (To stay up to date with the growing world of DV and Firewire, get a subscription to my favorite mag of the moment, Res.Subscribe at www.resmag.com.)

STEP 01

one-stop CAPTURE

Other capture cards will work, but most of them use JPEG compression and, unless you go for the higher-priced cards, the quality, in my experience, isn't as good.

I achieved two goals by recording Christina with my digital video camera: First, because I've got a decent microphone on my camera, I got a pretty good audio track, and second, I also captured visual imagery I was able to later incorporate in the spot.

Because I captured the audio and video together, it was necessary for me to bring them both into Premiere and export the audio as a separate track. Then, using methods previously described in Chapter 4, "Hillmancurtis.com Navigation," I selected the relevant video frames as bitmaps.

Exporting the audio in Premiere is pretty straightforward:

1 In Premiere, open your video clip by choosing File > Open. The clip appears in the monitor window as shown in figure 07:01.

2 Choose File > Export and select Audio from the drop-down menu (see figure 07:02).

figure **07:01**

figure **07:02**

continues

figure **07:03**

3 The Export Audio palette will appear. Name your file and select the Settings tab to change any of the settings for the file.

From my file, I exported the entire project at 44k, 16-bit stereo (see figure 07:03)—the rule being to start with the highest quality audio possible and apply compression later.

optimizing audio—
NORMALIZING

The next step is to open the exported audio in an audio wave-editing tool.

At hillmancurtis.com, we use SoundForge XP4.5 on Windows systems and SoundEdit 16 on Macs, but there are many decent digital audio software-processing packages available. CoolEdit Pro and Steinberg's WaveLab 2.0 come to mind. Just make sure that the software you use is capable of applying two very important functions for processing voiceovers: normalizing and applying noise gates.

Normalizing audio evens out the highs and lows of an audio signal. SoundForge normalizes a file by raising its volume so that the highest-level sample in the file reaches a user-specified level. In real life, normalizing an audio clip takes a fair amount of experimentation and practice. I recommend wearing headphones while trying different values. To normalize an audio file in SoundForge, follow these steps:

1 Open the file into the sound editor.

continues

2

With the whole clip selected, choose Process > Normalize, as shown in figure 07:04.

To normalize a file means to raise its volume so that the highest-level sample in the file reaches a user-defined level. I use this function to make sure I am fully utilizing the dynamic range available.

3

Adjust the slider to the desired level. What you want here is the biggest wave form, or loudest signal, without hearing any distortion. It usually takes me a few tries before I reach that point (see figure 07:05).

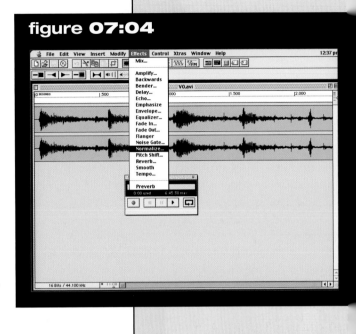

figure **07:04**

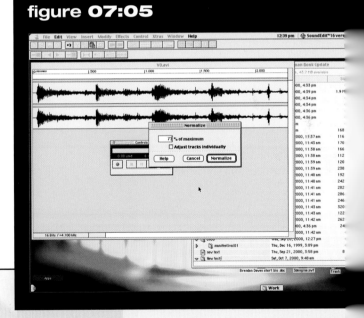

figure **07:05**

STEP 03

optimizing audio—
NOISE GATES

The natural rhythm of speaking and reading often brings a fair number of pauses into a voiceover. Unless you are recording in a professional sound booth, you'll pick up a great deal of ambient noise during a pause. That ambient noise is distracting and always seems to get louder during MP3 (or ACDM, for that matter) encoding. Although it's possible to edit out all the pauses, that process tends to also remove the natural cadences of speech—particularly important in the example voiceover, a poem. A better solution for handling noise during pauses is to apply an effect known as a noise gate. A *noise gate* takes all sound below a set threshold and totally attenuates it, reducing the audio to silence. In SoundForge, you can set how fast the gate opens and closes, thus affecting how the sound fades out and back in on either side of the silenced portion. Again, applying a noise gate takes practice and experimentation to achieve the right effect without clipping the surrounding audio.

To apply a noise gate in SoundForge, follow these steps:

1 With the whole clip selected, choose Effects > Noise Gate.

2 Adjust the Threshold so that it is just below the maximum sample rate, as shown in figure 07:06.

To find the maximum sample rate, choose a voiceless region in the waveform and select Tools > Statistics. Make note of the Maximum Sample Value; in the Noise Gate dialog, set the Threshold to a value a bit below the Maximum Sample Value.

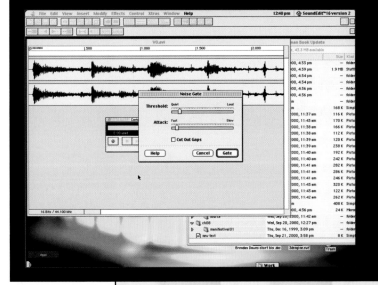

figure 07:06

3 If desired, enter new values for the Attack and Release times. What you want to end up with is simple; reduce the amount of low-level static and noise that occurs in the pauses between the reader speaking.

When it comes time to export the file as a .wav or .aif file, you might consider exporting it in pieces. For longer Flash movies, it's often easier to sync several different clips to onscreen imagery when working with sections. With the example file, I made an early decision to export it in four pieces. Why? With my recording, I felt it would be easier to work with and, with the use of the Smart Preload technique, better sync my audio to my visuals. Again, it all comes down to testing.

STEP 04

exporting audio
SECTIONS

To export your audio in sections, follow these steps:

1 Select a portion of the audio file. Find a natural break—a pause or a breath—where you can make a clean cut (see figure 07:07).

2 Copy the selection.

3 Open a new document by choosing File > New and then choose Edit > Paste.

4 Save the new file as either a .wav file (PC) or an .aif file (Mac).

5 Repeat this process until you have your entire audio track cut up into sequential segments and saved.

figure 07:07

STEP 05

encoding MP3 audio
IN FLASH

Having decided that I would target the voiceover as the most important element of this spot, I imported it into Flash first. That way I would have the voiceover to design to. When bringing sound into Flash—MP3 or otherwise—there's no need to create a symbol first. The Import command automatically recognizes the file type as a sound and inserts the file in the Library with an appropriate icon. You do, however, need to specify the Export type to enable MP3 encoding.

To import a sound and set it to MP3, follow these steps:

1 Choose File > Import and select the desired .wav or .aif file.

2 Open the Library window and select the imported audio file.

3 Select the Properties button at the bottom of the Library window (see figure 07:08).

4 From the Compression drop-down list, choose MP3.

The MP3 settings (Preprocessing, Bit Rate, and Quality) are activated.

figure 07:08

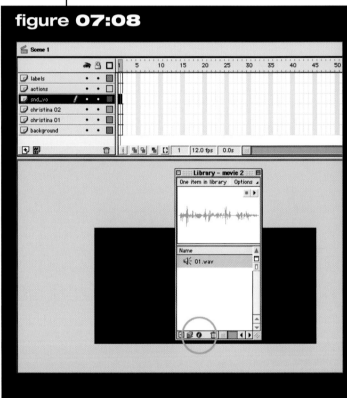

5 Select the desired Bit Rate and Quality from the drop-down lists (see figure 07:09).

You'll need to do a fair amount of testing to determine the best combination of bit rate and quality that still gives you a decent file size. For the example file, I found I could go to a bit rate of 32Kbps and Best quality. Under other circumstances, the high file size (65k) would normally be a terrifying figure, but I can ignore that because of the effect of streaming.

6 Convert a stereo clip to mono by enabling the Preprocessing option, if desired. Again, you need to ask yourself whether it's worth extra seconds on the download to have stereo playback. Mono will be a lighter file.

7 Click OK when you're satisfied with the sound settings.

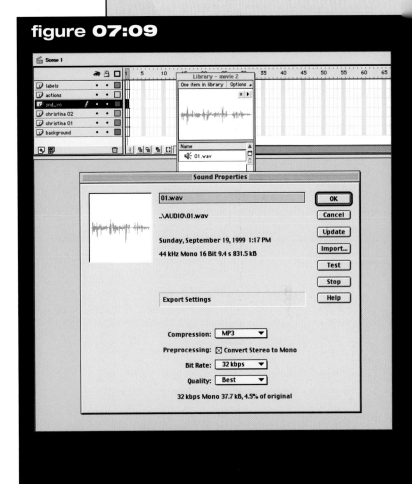

figure 07:09

applying global
EXPORT SETTINGS

The preceding procedure is used for individual clips, but Flash also has the capability to specify one setting for all clips in a movie. To choose one export setting for all your audio clips, follow these steps:

1 Choose File > Publish Settings.

2 In the Flash tab of the Publish Settings dialog, click the Set button next to Audio Stream and then follow the procedure outlined in the previous steps 4 through 6.

Use Publish Settings to apply global audio encoding—but only if your audio all comes from the same source.

3 Select the Override Sound Settings option (see figure 07:10). This will allow your publish settings to override any individual compression settings you may have applied to sounds in the library.

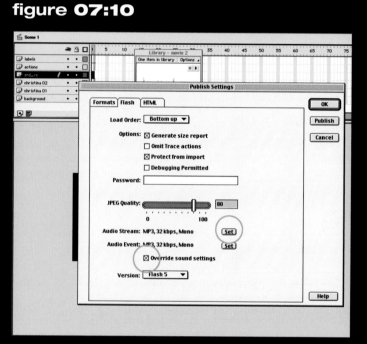

figure 07:10

In the example file, I can use this feature because all my audio comes from the same master source, Christina's reading; if, however, the movie mixed sound from a variety of sources—effects, voice-overs, and so on—I wouldn't apply the settings globally.

STEP 07

integrating visuals and STREAMING AUDIO

While encoding audio as an MP3 stream is fairly straightforward in Flash, syncing the audio with the video tracks is trickier. Placement on the Timeline of both the audio and visual elements is key. It's also important not to exceed performance expectations; for example, it's currently not possible to synchronize lip movement and audio on all systems, over all bandwidths. Keeping those restrictions in mind, you'll find a host of techniques that serve your movie more creatively than a strict 1:1 correspondence between audio and visual imagery.

To insert an audio track into your movie, follow these steps:

1 In a new layer, place a keyframe in the desired location.

2 Select the Sound Panel. If the Sound Panel is not visible, choose Window > Panels > Sound.

3 From the Sound pull-down menu, select your audio file.

4 From the Sync drop-down list, select the Stream option (see figure 07:11).

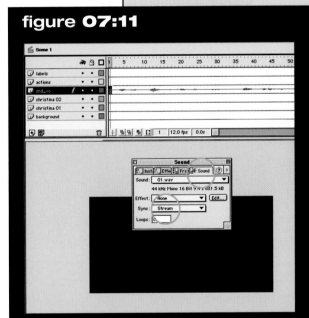

figure **07:11**

continues

5 If necessary, add additional frames in your movie Timeline so that the audio clip is visible on the Timeline in its entirety (see figure 07:12).

When designing your movie in Flash, streaming brings one major advantage to the production table: scrubbing. *Scrubbing* is the ability to hear audio or see video as you drag the playhead across the frames. Scrubbing the sound makes it easier to sync visual text to aural text.

After all of the audio clips are imported and laid out in the Timeline, the balance of the work is to make the movie visually attractive. To do this I fade in a mixture of text phrases and bitmaps that sync with the audio. In *Sky*, I use—and reuse—three visual elements: a picture of the poet, reading, raising and lowering her head as she does so; a small (seven-frame) sequence of a person walking; and finally, the text phrases. With the text phrases I tried to capture key words from the poem and either pop or slow fade them on in synch with the audio.

It's important when mixing any visual element with streaming audio to be aware of what streaming actually means. I try to keep a strong mental image of this fixed-size pipeline that is, again, largely occupied by the audio stream. This image reminds me that any visual elements I introduce will have to share that pipeline—which, in turn, helps me to restrict my visuals to the essentials.

What I do is use different perspectives of the same visuals to vary the composition, and keep the file size down. In *Sky*, for example, you'll notice several moments where I juxtapose a 1/4 screen-size shot of Christina reading with an over-sized subset of frames from the same image sequence. Basically, I am reusing the limited bitmaps I have and by using the Scale and Rotate tool, I either scale them up or down in an attempt to come up with interesting new perspectives as shown by the

figure **07:12**

figure **07:13**

sequence of figures 07:13, 07:14, and 07:15. It's really very simple…not a whole lot of technique here—just scale, positioning, and keyframes, with space between them. But if you can intuitively plug into a rhythm of changing perspective it can be pretty compelling.

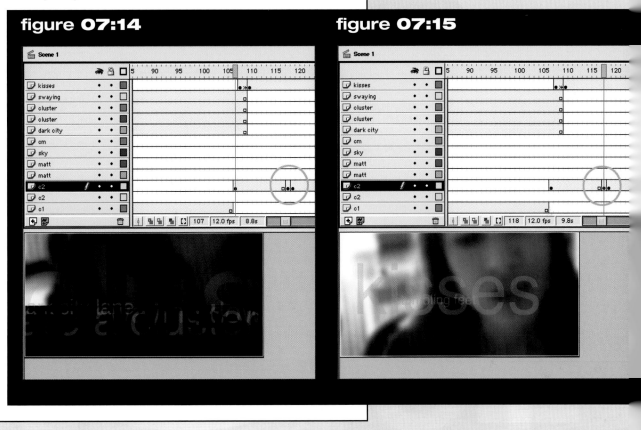

figure 07:14

figure 07:15

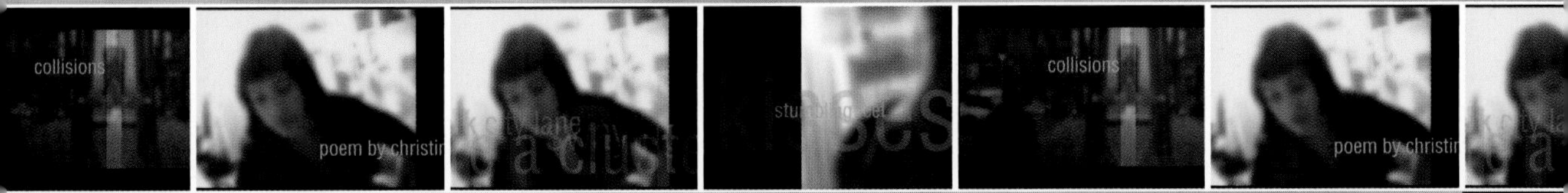

working the TEXT

With text, I tend to use simple, slow fades, which give me a bit of play in syncing with the audio cue. In *Sky*, particularly, I stayed away from zoom moves, both because the slower transitions were more in keeping with the work (a poem) and because zooms are very processor-intensive.

In *Sky*, many of the text phrases are handled in a similar three-step process:

- First, I bring the text in just a bit ahead of the audio cue and fade it up from an Alpha transparency of 12 to 100.

- Next, the text moves slightly to one side—around 10 pixels—so that it appears to be floating.

- Then, while the text is still moving, I reduce the Alpha transparency to 12.

Why do I bring the text in and out at 12 rather than zero? Again, the two worlds of visual composition and file functionality coincide for me. Limiting the Alpha blends to a smaller range reduces processor usage and leaving the text on-screen, in a very subtle manner, adds texture to the scene and enhances the visual for me.

To re-create the use of text phrases in *Sky*, follow these steps:

1 Use the playhead to scrub the audio and find where the phrase is spoken as shown in figure 07:16. (If you don't hear anything as you move the play-head, make sure the sound sync is set to Stream within Frame properties.)

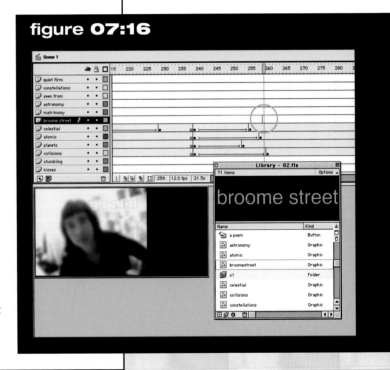

figure 07:16

2 Insert a new layer to hold the text element.

3 Create a new graphic symbol by choosing Insert > New Symbol or using the keyboard shortcut Ctrl-F8 / Cmd-F8 and label it the same as the text.

In my example, I use the phrase Broome Street.

4 Use the Text tool to make the text phrase within that graphic symbol.

I tend to use a single font with no more than two colors for all the text in a movie. In *Sky*, the primary variable was text size with a range from 11 to 44 points, while the font I chose was Helvetica.

5 In the primary scene, create a keyframe (using the keyboard shortcut F6) just slightly prior to when the audio phrase is spoken.

6 Drag an instance of the phrase from the Library to the stage and position where you want it to appear. Time your synced text phrases to appear slightly before the spoken phrase is heard (see figure 07:17).

7 Create a second keyframe 20 frames after the initial text keyframe.

figure 07:17

continues

8 Select the first keyframe, which in turn selects the instance of your text on the stage. Next choose the Effect Panel.

9 In the Effect Panel, choose Alpha as the effect type and reduce the Alpha to 12.

10 While the first keyframe is still selected, choose Insert > Create Motion Tween.

The phrase Broome Street is introduced in a slow fade up, syncing perfectly with the voiceover.

Now I will leave the phrase onstage until the phrase "Broome Street" has been spoken and then I'll fade it back out, moving the text to the right slightly as it fades out to give it the sensation of floating.

the fade and
FLOAT OUT

For the fade and float out, follow these steps:

1 Create a third keyframe (using the keyboard shortcut F6) just slightly prior to the audio phrase ending.

2 Create a fourth and final keyframe 20 frames after the third keyframe.

3 Reposition the final text element to the right by a small amount (approximately 7 pixels) by selecting the text object and then pressing the right arrow key (7 times) to move the element horizontally to the right. If you use the mouse to drag the object, you might position the text slightly up or down and the "floating to one side" illusion will be altered.

continues

4 While the final keyframe is selected, choose the Effect Panel.

5 In the Effect Panel, reduce the Alpha to 12.

6 Select any frame between the third and fourth keyframes and choose Insert > Create Motion Tween (see figure 07:18).

The text will now float to one side, fading as it goes.

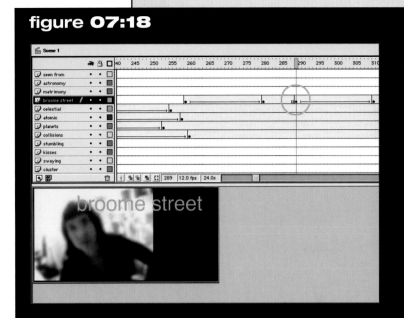

figure 07:18

STEP 10

smart preloads and
TESTING THE STREAM

While designing, I need to periodically check the pipeline. To do this I will employ the bandwidth profiler. We have gone over this already in Chapter 3, "20k Advertisement," but it's crucial for this file and any other file that incorporates streaming audio, so let's quickly revisit the process:

1 Choose Control > Test Movie.

Flash generates a .swf file and plays it within the authoring environment. Choose View > 100% to view your movie at 100%.

2 Press Enter / Return to stop the movie.

continues

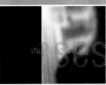

3 If necessary, select a new modem setting from the Control menu.

4 Select Control > Rewind to make sure you're at the start of your movie.

5 Choose View > Bandwidth Profiler or use the keyboard shortcut Ctrl-B / Cmd-B.

Flash draws a bar graph depicting the streaming assets. Elements that appear above the red line indicate a problem, where the assets weigh more (the file is bigger) than the streaming can comfortably support.

6 Select Control > Show Streaming or use the keyboard shortcut Ctrl-Enter / Cmd-Return).

As the movie plays, the green indicator bar shows the state of the streaming, whereas the playhead indicates which frame is being played. Ideally, you want the streaming indicator to be just ahead of the playhead at all times while invoking the shortest preload time possible. Avoid situations where the playhead catches up to the stream and must wait for more material to load, as shown in figure 07:19.

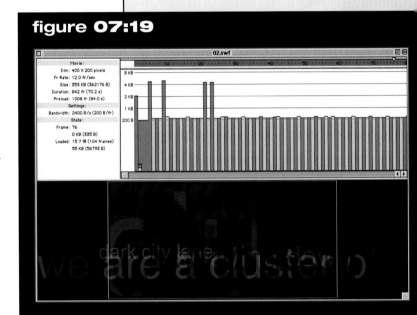

figure 07:19

smart PRELOADS

When I test the file, I notice that the playhead does indeed catch up to the stream, and does so right in the middle of one of Christina's phrases. So it just sort of cuts her off mid-sentence. By placing a couple of smart preloads we can control the stream and decide on good places for the presentation to pause and preload assets, thus avoiding sudden interruptions.

1 In the label layer, add a keyframe on frame 1.

2 Click the keyframe and then select the Frame Panel.

3 In the Label field, enter **01**.
A label named 01 is inserted.

4 Repeat steps 1–3 on frame 3 to create a label named Start.

5 Repeat steps 1–3 on frame 27 to create a label named Load (see figure 07:20).

6 In the action layer, double-click the keyframe in frame 1 to open the Frame Actions window.

7 From the Basic Actions list, double-click the If Frame Is Loaded action.

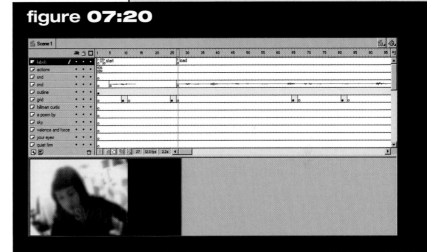

figure **07:20**

continues

8 In the Type drop-down list, choose Frame Label and select Load fron the Frame drop-down on the right-hand side.

9 Double-click Go To from the Basic Actions list.

10 Make sure the Go To and Play option is checked at the bottom of the window.

11 From the Type drop-down, choose the Frame Label option and then choose Start from the Frame drop-down on the right-hand side. Close the window when you're done.

For this action to work properly, another loop must be added.

12 In the action layer, add another keyframe to frame 2 and double-click it to open the Frame Actions window.

13 Add a Go To action and specify the 01 label. Make sure the Go To and Play option is checked. This creates a loop that sends the playhead back to the script in frame 1, until that script returns a positive.

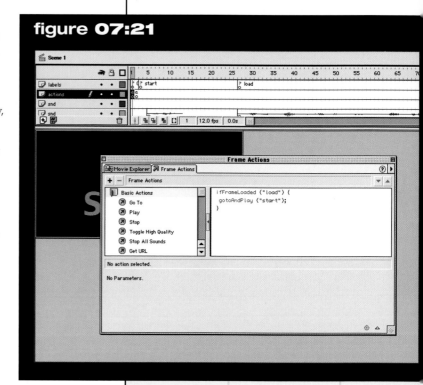

figure **07:21**

When I test the movie, I still get an interruption midway through the file. So I write another preload action, choosing a pause in Christina's delivery as the spot to preload (see figure 07:22). Now, if you view this movie on a DSL, cable modem, or T1 these preload scripts will be read, but will return a positive immediately. In other words, they will basically be invisible and cause no hesitation in the playback. However, if you view the movie on a 56.6, there will be a 2-second pause at the start and another 2- to 4-second pause about a third of the way through. That second pause is placed in a natural pause of Christina's delivery, so it's not that noticeable. Once past that pause, enough of the file is preloaded to stream perfectly to the end.

figure 07:22

conclusion

So, the trick to this file is more conceptual than technical, really. As long as I entered into it with a clear visualization of my pipeline I could pull it off. Identifying the voiceover as the most important element in the file, as the star of this spot, was the most important step. It allowed me to shoot for the best audio quality and have a reference point for the visual support. Utilizing MP3 compression was a key as well. MP3 gave me a superior audio quality with a lighter file and with a better stream. The fact that I chose to stream the audio, accepting that there might be situations in which a visual frame or two might be dropped was paramount and I designed visuals and moves accordingly.

EIGHT

about manifestival   about the films   view films 1 2 3   interactive cinema   supporters/party info

MANIFESTIVAL

08:08:08

> "We worked in tandem to create a site we regard as one of our best. It's urban, with its shots of subways, mysterious, and a little dark.

interactive cinema   supporters/public info

08: 01

thoughts

BEHIND THE DESIGN

Kiley Bates is a New York new media producer who came to us with her idea for an online film festival, ManiFestival. The moment she first described her vision for it, we were on board. ManiFestival would be a site done in Flash that would showcase independent digital film and video shorts. Recognizing the awesome potential the web offers for online distribution of short digital films, we knew we had to be involved. Kiley expressed her desire for a site that would both reflect the artistic focus of ManiFestival and be a functional…quick-download, navigationally quick…design.

Hillmancurtis.com's art director Ian Kovalik and I worked in tandem to create a site we regard as one of our best. It's urban, with its shots of subways, mysterious, and a little dark. The problem was that after we had designed it, its performance was not up to our standards. The subway shots, taken from video, were heavy and slow to download and that affected the user experience, since the user couldn't interact with the site until everything was downloaded.

What we decided to do was to try to structure the site so that the essential elements, the interface, and the navigational elements would download first. This is crucial because we wanted to give the user immediate access to all areas of the site. Once the interface and navigational buttons were downloaded and functional (roughly three seconds on 56.6), the heavy subway footage would be downloaded in the background.

It was easy to come to this decision. The hard part was going to be pulling it off. For this, we turned to Fred Sharples of Orange Design. Fred and I have a long history of working together, and his company, Orange Design, has established itself as the preeminent shop for Flash 4 programming as well as Macromedia Generator programming.

After I saw what Fred and his team came up with for the ManiFestival site, I decided I had to include it in this book. This chapter offers insight into the mind of one of the leaders in Flash programming. That said, I'll turn you over to Fred.

Flash object-oriented programming

Before we get into the code of the ManiFestival, I think it's important to convey a few principles of the Flash 4 programming environment. Flash 4 action scripts become elegant when looked at with the notion of object-oriented programming (OOP) in mind. The concept is simple and you don't need to have programming experience to understand its principles.

In OOP jargon, an object is an individual module of a program. These self-contained modules are designed so that they can be used—and most importantly, reused—in various programming projects. An object becomes a building block, which, by design, increases your productivity. It can also make it easy to add and remove features from a larger project without breaking the entire architecture. It can also be much easier to track down problems in the code when designed properly.

How does OOP relate to Flash? In essence, Flash movies are objects, as are Flash movie clips (see figure 08:01).

Each movie clip is a self-contained module that can be referenced, control other objects, and manipulate portions of the overall movie. The following shows some of the key features of objects in Flash:

- Objects in Flash have their own Timelines (see figure 08:02). The individual Timeline gives a Flash object its independence from the overall Timeline, as is evident in embedded movies and movie clips.

- Objects can tell each other where to go in each other's Timelines (see figure 08:03). Using the 'with' function, which is similar to the Tell Target command in Flash 4, one object can specify which frame in another object is next—and whether that frame should play or stop. This is a very important feature that lies at the heart of Flash object-oriented programming.

- Objects have properties (see figure 08:04). Just as objects in life have properties—an orange, for example, has the properties of size, color, taste, and aroma—so do Flash objects. A Flash object's properties include scale, position, alpha, visibility, and rotation. The Flash code for setting the rotation of an object labeled "orange" to 30 degrees would look like that shown in figure 08:05.

figure 08:01

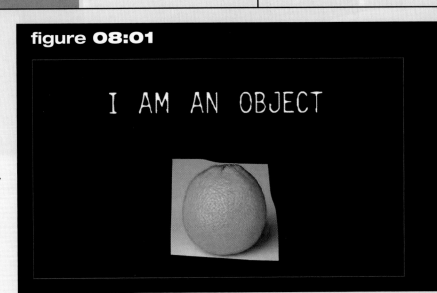

figure 08:02

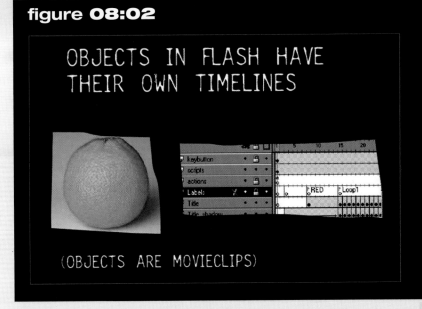

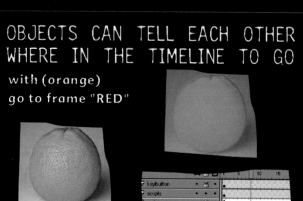

OBJECTS CAN TELL EACH OTHER
WHERE IN THE TIMELINE TO GO
with (orange)
go to frame "RED"

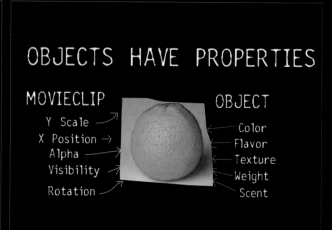

OBJECTS HAVE PROPERTIES

MOVIECLIP   OBJECT
  Y Scale   Color
  X Position →   Flavor
  Alpha   Texture
  Visibility   Weight
  Rotation   Scent

- Objects have their own storage containers, called *variables*. A variable acts as a temporary storage container, which can be accessed from other objects or affect the current object (see figure 08:06). For example, you might want to store a user's name in a variable called bestfriend.

bestfriend = "Sally";

Now you've stored the name and you can use it throughout the movie without checking the name every time the screen changes.

Anything can be put in a variable. In Flash, a variable can hold any type of data—numbers or text (also known as *integers* and *strings*). Unlike as in other languages, in Flash you don't have to declare a variable to be an integer or a string before using it.

Variables can be named anything you want. The easiest way to get the most out of object-oriented programming is to name your variables usefully. It's difficult to keep track of what var01, var02, and var03 do—however, it's hard to miss what thePosition, isOffScreen and isHit intend.

OBJECTS CAN CHANGE
EACH OTHER'S PROPERTIES

_root.orange._rotation = 30

- Any object can change what is inside another object's variables (see figure 08:07). Not only can variables be set as part of the overall movie, but one object can alter another object's variables. This facility allows for advanced interactivity. Suppose that you have a skiing game where you have a skier, the "skier" object. When the skier object collides with a "tree" object, the skier object sets a variable called score in an object called scoreboard.

  `_root.scoreboard.score = –50;`

- One object can be nested inside another object. Just as one symbol can be composed of other symbols in Flash, one object can be composed of other objects. In fact, that's the essence of OOP.

- Objects can use hierarchies (see figure 08:08). When one object is inside another, together they're in a hierarchical relationship, just like a folder and subfolder:

  `meta_orange.orange.sub_orange`

figure **08:06**

YOU CAN SAVE ALL KINDS OF STUFF IN OBJECTS

variableS

bestfriend="sally"

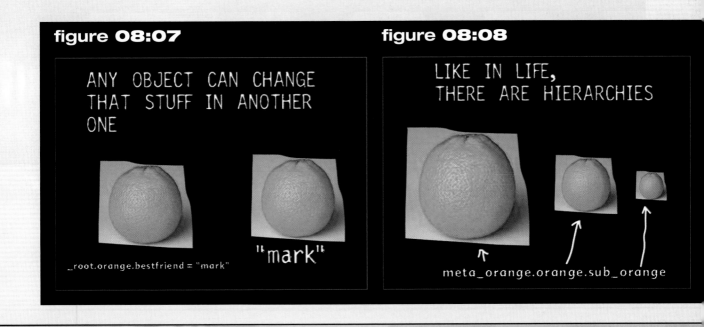

figure **08:07**

ANY OBJECT CAN CHANGE THAT STUFF IN ANOTHER ONE

"mark"

_root.orange.bestfriend = "mark"

figure **08:08**

LIKE IN LIFE, THERE ARE HIERARCHIES

meta_orange.orange.sub_orange

- Objects address one another through these hierarchies (see figure 08:09). They do this using what we call 'dot syntax'. For example, if one object wanted to tell another object to go to a different frame, you might see Flash action code like this:

```
with (meta_orange) {
        do something
};
```

However, if you wanted to address another object contained within the meta_orange object, you would call it this way:

```
with (meta_orange.orange) {
do something
};
```

The dot tells ActionScript that you are addressing the object orange, which is an object in the object meta_orange.

You can even address an object that contains the current object by going up a level, like this:

```
with (_parent) {
do something
};
```

_parent is a special name built into Flash, which allows you to specify the object that contains the current object (i.e., 'above' the current object).

To address an object on the uppermost level, on the main Timeline, use_root:

```
with (_root.meta_orange) {
        do something
};
```

In this case, the meta_orange object is on the top level, and we call the top level using the _root locator.

In fact, you can address the main Timeline alone using:

```
with (_root)
```

The main Timeline can always be accessed using _root.

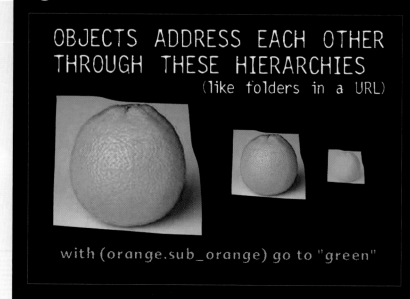

figure **08:09**

OBJECTS ADDRESS EACH OTHER THROUGH THESE HIERARCHIES
(like folders in a URL)

with (orange.sub_orange) go to "green"

Just as we use the hierarchy to address a with function, we can use the hierarchy to address variables and set properties in each other's objects.

Use the following to set an object's property:

```
meta_orange.orange.sub_orange._rotation = 179;
```

In this case, the sub_orange object would turn 179 degrees (about a half of a turn) on the screen when you set its rotation property.

Use the following to set a variable in an object:

```
meta_orange.orange.myColor = "green";
```

Setting the variable to green doesn't change anything on the screen. I simply set the storage container "myColor" to contain the word green.

Later I might use that word in another part of my code:

```
If (myColor == "green"){
    gotoAndStop ("green");
}
```

That's your primer for Flash 5 programming and architecture for now. Let's drop into the ManiFestival movie to see how to use this knowledge in a real-life example.

manifestival in
DEPTH

In creating the ManiFestival movie, the first step was to break out the movie into objects. In this relatively simple example, I look at what needs to move and change programmatically.

creating objects

The ManiFestival movie has five things that need to be controlled by ActionScript:

Dancer
Line
Logo
Subway
Tunnel

There are also three buttons: About ManiFestival, About the Films, and Featured Animation (see figure 08:10). These buttons control each of the five objects via Rollover and Rollout scripts.

figure **08:10**

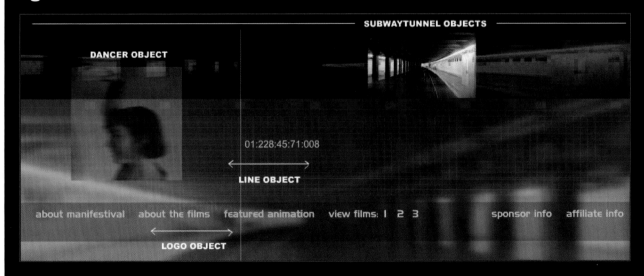

SUBWAYTUNNEL OBJECTS

DANCER OBJECT

01:228:45:71:008

LINE OBJECT

about manifestival   about the films   featured animation   view films: 1 2 3   sponsor info   affiliate info

LOGO OBJECT

continues

I need to make each of the objects into movie clips so I can talk to them via ActionScript. We don't need to go into great detail on each of these, but let's have a look at each one and what it contains.

the dancer object

The Dancer movie clip consists of a series of video images of a pirouette (see figure 08:11). The first part of the sequence labeled "start" has three frames spaced at three-frame intervals showing the first quarter turn of the pirouette. The second part of the sequence is labeled "one" and shows the next half-turn of the pirouette in three-frame intervals. The next sequence, labeled "two," is the last quarter-turn of the sequence and again is in three-frame intervals.

Following this sequence is another sequence called "spin," consisting of the first half of the pirouette but with only one image per frame, making it much faster than the earlier sequence. The last sequence is called "spin2" and is the last half of this faster pirouette, again at one-frame intervals.

the line object

The Line object is a movie clip containing a vertical line, a sequence of numbers alongside it, and a sound clip (see figure 08:12). As the movie clip plays, the line moves horizontally to the left. The numbers change and follow the line horizontally. A small ambient sound clip plays. This movie clip does not contain any labels. There are Stop actions at the beginning and end of the Timeline.

figure 08:11

figure 08:12

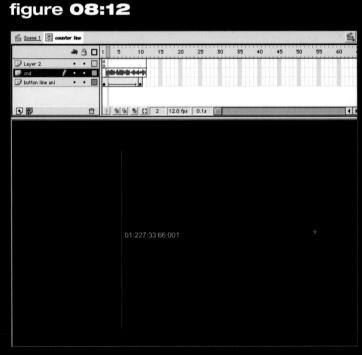

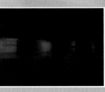

the logo object

The Logo object is a movie clip that contains the word ManiFestival (see figure 08:13). The word moves across the screen from right to left and fades out to 0 alpha transparency.

There are 41 frames in this movie clip. One label, called Start, is in this clip. There is a stop action at the end of the Timeline.

figure **08:13**

manifestival

continues

STEP 02

naming the INSTANCES

After these movie clips are created, I give them each an instance name. An instance name becomes the name of the movie clip for all of your programming. That is what is used to identify your clip in paths such as Tell Target and Set Variable. The name of your clip in the library is not important. It can be different from your instance name. In some cases, you might use the same clip over and over again but have a different instance name for each copy.

To create an instance name, follow these steps:

1 Select the Timeline in your main movie and insert a new layer.

2 Name the layer.
I use the name of the object that will go in the layer—for instance, Dancer.

3 Open the Library.

4 Select the movie clip you want to use. In this case, select "Dancer."

5 Drag the movie clip to the screen.

6 Select the newly added Movie Clip.

7 Select the Instance Panel.

8 In the Instance Name text field, enter the desired Instance Name; dancer.

figure 08:14

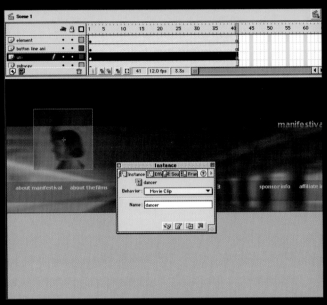

Now you can address this movie clip from anywhere in your movie. For instance, in this example, we tell the Dancer object to play from its start label:

```
with (_root.dancer) {
gotoAndPlay ("start");
}
```

DECONSTRUCTION

STEP 03

external movie clip objects—the tunnel and SUBWAY MOVIE CLIPS

As Hillman described earlier, one of the challenges of this project was to make a large movie work well and react immediately for users with slower modem connections.

To address the file-loading issue, we looked at the largest animations: the subway and tunnel animations (see figures 08:15 and 08:16).

These two clips are different from the others in that they will be separate files existing outside of the main movie. The reason that you have these files outside of the main movie is that they are relatively large—around 21k each. Although that seems small, users on modems will experience a noticeable delay that could interfere with their experience.

To solve the problem, I decided to make them separate files and load them programmatically using the load movie command. The movie then became three Flash movies with three SWF files. The main movie will load before the subway and tunnel movies, thus showing the user the main interface very quickly. This modular approach is especially useful when creating large interactive movies such as Flash web sites and adventure games where one wants to load only a few movies at a time.

Usually when creating clips that load on the fly, it's easier to create the clips in their main parent movie, in this case ManiFestival. This makes it much easier to lay out your clip and make adjustments to it.

figure 08:15

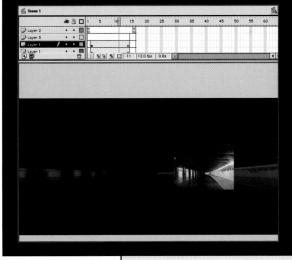

figure 08:16

continues

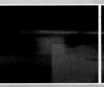
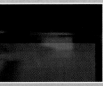

1 Create your movie clip in your movie just like any other movie clip: Select the frame, choose Modify > Instance and then click the Movie Clip option.

In this case your movie clip is called subway.

2 Select the entire Timeline of your subway movie clip.

3 Select Edit > Copy Frames (Ctrl-Alt-C / Cmd-Option-C).

4 Create a new movie.

5 Select Modify > Movie and set the movie properties to be the same as your original "parent" movie. The size and frame rate are very important.

6 Select the first frame in your new Timeline.

7 Select Edit > Paste Frames.

8 Save the file, naming it **Subway.fla**.

9 Select File > Export Movie (and save as .SWF.

10 Now go back to your original ManiFestival movie and open the subway movie clip.

11 Delete all the keyframes. Then delete all the layers, leaving one empty keyframe in the movie clip.

Now the Subway movie clip in your original movie becomes a container (see figure 08:17). You load the new file subway.swf into it later. Leave the empty container on the main Timeline, though. You'll see the empty movie clip represented by a small white circle (see figure 08:18).

Repeat the previous steps 1–11 to create the Tunnel object. Export the movie as an .SWF (choose File > Export Movie) and save as **tunnel.swf**.

figure 08:17

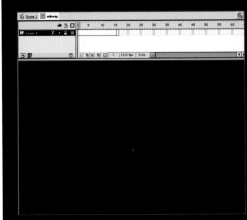

figure 08:18

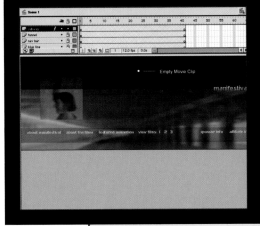

the script OBJECT

Next, I'm going to present a special kind of object. I call this the Script object. The Script object will contain most of your ActionScripts and variables. Think of it as the master control for the entire movie. Putting all your actions and variables in one place makes it easy to find and fix programming mistakes.

I'm also going to introduce ActionScript functions. A function is a piece of code that can be used anywhere in your movie. For example, we can write a function that increases the width of a movie clip:

```
function clipFatter(clipName) {
                         _root[clipName]._width =
_root[clipName]._width + 10
}
```

Each time we wanted to increase the width of the movie clip by 10, say when a button is clicked, we would 'call' the function like this:

```
on (release) {
clipFatter("myClip");
}
```

Notice when we call the function, we pass the name of the clip to the function, which in this case is myClip. You can see how functions are incredibly flexible—this same piece of code can be used on whatever movie clip we specify, without having to write separate code for each clip! Remember though: A function does nothing until it is invoked by calling it.

creating the script object

Follow these steps to create the Script object:

1 Insert a new layer at the top of your layers and label it **Scripts**.

2 Choose Insert > New Symbol (Ctrl-F8 / Cmd-F8) and select Movie Clip as its behavior. Name the symbol **Scripts**.

continues

After the symbol is created, Flash automatically opens the Symbol Editor; no object or graphic is placed on the Scripts stage, however. All the work is inserted as an action.

3 Double-click the first keyframe to open the Frame Actions Panel.

4 In the next step, we're going to start to write our functions on the one and only frame of the script movie clip. Even though all the functions will reside in frame 1 of the Script movie clip, the scripts will do nothing until they are called from elsewhere in our movie.

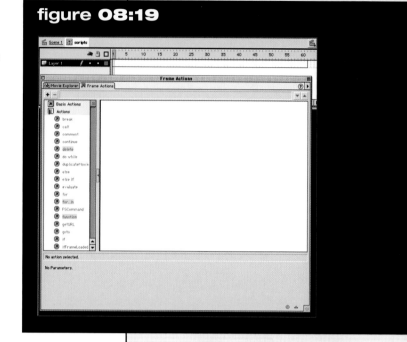

figure 08:19

the script object:
INITIALIZE SCRIPT

The Initialize script in the Script movie clip is the script that gets called before anything else in the movie. In the ManiFestival movie, we use the Initialize function to load the Subway and Tunnel movies.

To create the Initialize script, follow these steps:

1 Open the Script movie clip from the Library.

2 Open the Library and Select the Scripts movie clip.

3 Double-click to open.

continues

4 On the first frame, double-click it to open the Frame Actions Panel.

5 Make sure you're in Expert Mode in the Frame Actions Panel by pressing Ctrl-E / Cmd-E.

6 Type the following to first define the function:

function initialize() {

};

7 Now position your cursor on the line between the curly brackets of the function. All of our code for the function fits in here.

8 Now type:

loadMovie
("tunnel.swf",
_root.tunnel);

This loads the movie "tunnel.swf" into the target that we've defined as _root tunnel. Remember, _root refers to the main Timeline.

9 Repeat the above step to load the second movie. For ManiFestival, subway.swf is loaded into target_root.subway.

When you're finished, your initializing functions should look like this:

function initialize() {
loadMovie ("tunnel.swf",_root.tunnel);
loadMovie ("subway.swf",_root.subway);
}

figure 08:20

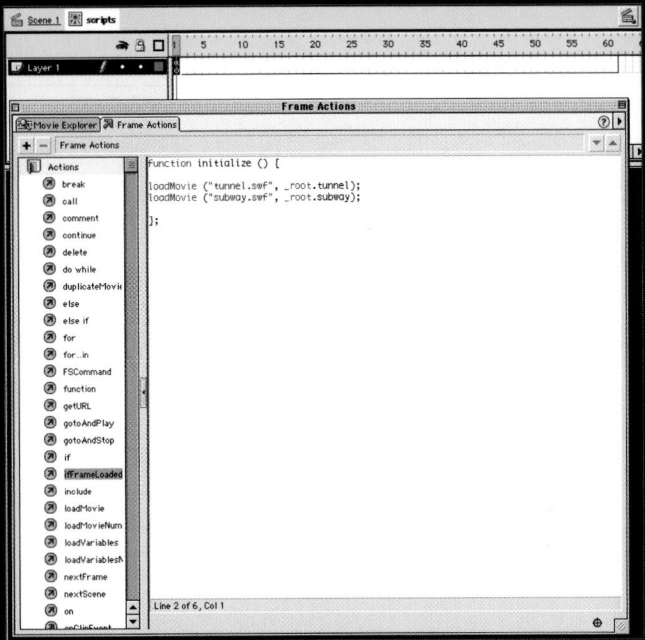

continues

NOTE load variables

In the Load Movie dialog, you'll notice an option called Load Variables. I didn't need to use the Load Variables option for this example, but it's a powerful new function you should be aware of.

With this, a set of variables is passed from the location listed in the URL field, which allows the server to dynamically update a Flash movie. Or, more specifically, it allows a Flash movie to update itself from the server-side script by calling it. When these options are used, the URL location is typically a CGI or other server-side script. It can also refer to an external text file. Variables returned from a server-side script or text file are listed in URL encoded strings. Consider the following:

"myvariable=100&myvariable2=test &myvariable3=ok"

By calling this server-side script or text file, the variables myvariable, myvariable2, and myvariable3 are now set to "100," "test," and "ok," respectively, in your movie.

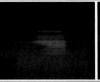

STEP 06

create an instance of the
SCRIPT MOVIE CLIP

Just as we did for the Dancer, Line, and Logo movie clips, we will also create an instance of the Script movie clip.

1 Select the Timeline in your main movie and insert a new layer, naming it **Scripts**.

2 Open the Library and select the Scripts movie clip.

3 Drag the movie clip to the screen.

4 Double-click on the Scripts movie clip on the screen.

5 In the Instance Properties dialog, select the Movie Clip option.

6 In the Instance Name text box, enter **Scripts**. Press Enter / Return.

Notice that your Scripts object will also look like an empty circle, just like the empty Subway and Tunnel movie clips.

STEP 07

run the initialization
ROUTINE

The last—but vitally important—step is to run the initialization function from the main movie. This is simply a matter of calling the function. The playback head of the movie clip does not actually move; the function in the clip—in this case, scripts—is simply executed.

1 In the main Timeline, create a layer called **Actions**. Double-click the first keyframe of the Actions layer to open the Frame Actions Panel.

continues

2 Make sure the Frame Actions Panel is in Expert Mode by pressing Ctrl-E / Cmd-E.

3 Type the following:

scripts.initialize();

This executes or calls the initialize function inside the Script movie clip, as shown in figure 08:21.

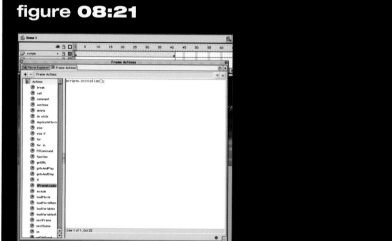

figure **08:21**

Now the main Timeline calls the initialization script and then loads the movies. The rest of the movie will work even when the Subway and Tunnel movies are still loading. If we kept the Subway and Tunnel movies in the main Timeline, we'd get stuck in the movie waiting for these large animations to load.

manifestival movie BEHAVIOR

We've looked at our objects and set up our initialization routines. Now let's look at the interactive elements of the movie. The movie interface is controlled by the three main navigation buttons: About ManiFestival, About the Films, and Featured Animation (see figure 08:22).

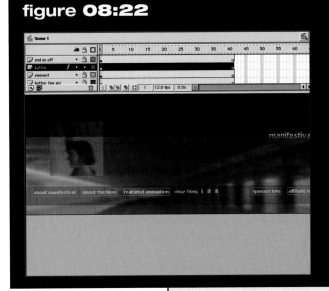

figure 08:22

When the user rolls over, rolls out, or clicks a button, different animations, such as the two large subway and tunnel animations, are triggered. Each button triggers a different sequence of animations and, in some cases, shows the animation in a different place.

On rollover, a movie clip showing a dancer spinning begins to play and a vertical line of text moves horizontally across the screen, above the button. The ManiFestival logo fades up and moves horizontally across the screen.

On rollout, the stopped movie clip dims and a larger movie clip plays, showing a subway station as it is passed.

about the films

On rollover, the Dancer movie clip plays from where it left off and the same line of text floats across the screen, above the second button. The logo repeats its movement across the screen.

On rollout, the spinning movie clip plays just a bit more and then stops while a different movie clip plays, showing a tunnel speeding past.

continues

featured animation

On rollover, the Dancer movie clip again picks up from where it last stopped while the text floats across the screen, above the third button. The logo repeats the same movement here as well.

On rollout, the spinning movie clip plays a bit more, as with the About the Films button, and then stops. Here, no additional movie clip plays.

What keeps the navigation intriguing is the combination of several similar elements, each adapted to a specific button. Of particular note is the way the movie clip of the dancer continues to play from its current position, instead of restarting each time it is called. This action—as well as that of the text line moving relative to a particular button—is controlled by object-oriented programming.

To handle such a complex set of behaviors, it is best to get organized. You have two goals in mind. One is to make the code as compact and reusable as possible. In other words, you want to combine all the behaviors into as few scripts as possible. The other goal is to break the movie apart into separate smaller manageable objects.

This combination of breaking apart and combining is best done on paper before you start. Programmers often draw out flow charts. You can simply draw boxes for each object and label them with variable names and behaviors of each object.

combining SCRIPTS

Now let's open up the Script object again and look at the other scripts. The Rollover script and Rollout script have been made into "generic" scripts. They can be called by every Navigation button, yet will do different things for each. Simply set a few variables that affect the Rollout or Rollover script, and they change the behavior of the script. The reason one does this becomes apparent in large projects that can change during the development process. Suppose a client wants all the buttons to show a logo on the screen on rollover. Instead of going through every button script in the project, you can simply change one line in one script. In huge projects this can save hours.

creating the generic rollover action

You need to plan carefully to get the most out of object-oriented programming. Typically, you'll have one or more general routines that are maintained in the scripts object. Each of these series of actions must be designed so that it can accept variables from other objects. The variables are, in essence, the details of the general routine. By changing the routine's variables before you call a routine, you can change how that general routine behaves.

In the ManiFestival movie, for example, there are two general routines: RolloverScript and RolloutScript. The RolloverScript performs three general actions (plays the Dancer movie, moves a line of simulated time-code, and floats the name of the festival across the screen) whereas the RolloutScript invokes two actions (plays the dancer movie again and plays a second movie). The particulars of these actions—what portion of the Dancer movie is played, where the time-code moves from and to, and which second movie plays—are set by the variables passed to the general routines when they are called from each separate button.

the rollover
SCRIPT

Follow these steps to re-create the RolloverScript:

1 Double-click the Scripts object in the Library to open the Symbol Editing window.

2 Double-click the first keyframe in the Timeline to open up the Frame Actions Panel. You should see our initialize function that we defined previously. We are now going to add another function for the RolloverScript. We can put as many functions as we like in the same frame; in fact, it's a good idea to keep them in the same place so you know where things are.

3 Define a new function called rolloverScript like this:

function rolloverScript() {

}

4 Position your cursor in the line between the curly brackets and then pick up from step 1 on the following section.

figure 08:23

the rollover script: controlling the LINE OBJECT

When creating a generic routine that affects more than one aspect of the movie, it's best to work on one area at a time. The first object I'll address is the line of simulated time-code, the Line object, that moves from right to left, above each button.

1 With this time code line, we need to change its X and Y position and then tell the line movie clip to play.

2 First, to change the X value, we type:

_root.line._x=line_x;

In this example, I first change the X Position property of the Line object to a variable line_x. You'll see later that when I call this function from the navigational buttons, I give the line_x variable a value. Each navigation button will set this value to a different number. This is what makes the code reusable and flexible.

3 Repeat step 2 for the Y Position property, with the same Target (_root.line) and line_y as the Value. When you're done, your Actions panel should look like the one in figure 08:24.

4 Using the with statement, type:

with (_root.line) {

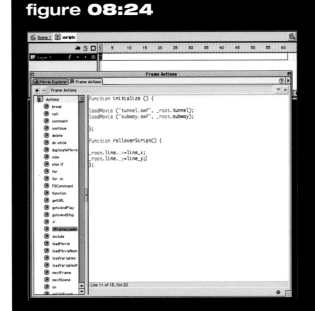

figure **08:24**

continues

5 On the next line type:

gotoAndPlay (2)

6 Finally, close the with statement with a curly bracket like this:

}

The _root.line object has a Stop action in frame 1, so going to frame 2 immediately plays the object.

The complete code for the first section of the RolloverScript looks like this:

```
_root.line._x=line_x;
_root.line._y=line_y;
with (_root.line) {
gotoAndPlay (2);
};
```

STEP 12

rolloverscript: controlling the DANCER MOVIE CLIP

The next portion of the RolloverScript affects the movie clip of the spinning dancer. The movie clip object is called /dancer, after the name of the performer. For this movie clip, two elements are important: the transparency and the portion of the clip being played. The movie clip is made more opaque when it plays and less opaque when it stops; the Alpha property handles transparency.

Because I want different buttons to play different portions of the movie clip, a variable is used in combination with the Go and Play action. This variable, dancer_framelabel, is set in each of the buttons. I also want to be sure that the first time the movie clip plays, it starts from the beginning. To base an action on a current property of an object, you use what is referred to, in programming jargon, as a *conditional* statement. One such conditional statement in Flash is the If-Else-End-If series: If my condition is met, do this action; else, do that one.

continues

Follow these steps to reconstruct the
Dancer Control in the RolloverScript:

1 If necessary, double-click
the first keyframe to enter the
Frame Actions Panel.

2 Following on from the last
with statement, alter the Alpha
level of the dancer object by
typing:

_root.dancer._alpha=66;

3 Now, when any rollover is
initiated, the _root.dancer
movie clip becomes more
opaque without overtaking the
screen. You want the Dancer
object to have this transparency
for every rollover. That is why
you set this property to a
value rather than a variable.

4 Using the with statement, enter the following line:

with (_root.dancer) {

You've identified the target, so it's time to begin to
enter the conditional statement. You want to create a
statement that acts one way if the current frame is
larger than 10 (meaning the movie is underway) and
another way if it's not.

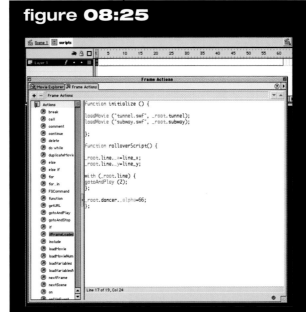

figure **08:25**

STEP 13

building a conditional statement in the EXPRESSION EDITOR

Using a conditional statement is a way of checking whether something is true or false. Usually we check the value of a variable. We can check whether the value is greater than, less than, equal to, or some combination of these. If the statement is true, we do one set of routines. If it is not, we do another. Here I'll show you how to check what frame the playback head is on in the Dancer Clip (see figure 08:26).

The Expression Editor allows you to build an expression from a preset list of available functions, properties, and operators. It's kind of like a library of built-in routines. This is the heart of Actions script.

figure 08:26

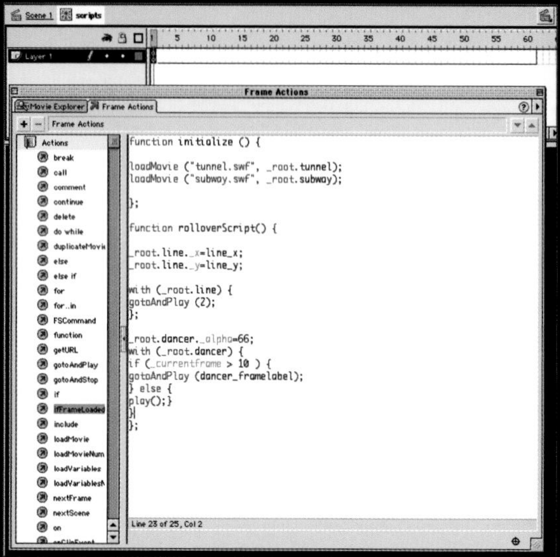

Scene 1
scripts
Frame Actions
Movie Explorer
Frame Actions
Actions
function initialize () {
loadMovie ("tunnel.swf", _root.tunnel);
loadMovie ("subway.swf", _root.subway);
};
function rolloverScript() {
_root.line._x=line_x;
_root.line._y=line_y;
with (_root.line) {
gotoAndPlay (2);
};
_root.dancer._alpha=66;
with (_root.dancer) {
if (_currentframe > 10) {
gotoAndPlay (dancer_framelabel);
} else {
play();}
}
};
Line 23 of 25, Col 2

1 On the line following the first line of the with statement, type:

if (_currentframe>10) {

The condition is contained inside the first set of brackets. The _currentframe property is the current frame of the movie clip. This is used to keep track of where the playback head is in the movie clip.

2 In this conditional statement, we want to see if the playback head is on a frame greater than 10.

3

On the following line, type:

gotoAndPlay (dancer_framelabel)

The dancer_framelabel variable will be set by the various buttons calling the RolloverScript. The _root.dancer movie clip has a series of labels for different frames.

Next we need to finish this part of the condition by closing the curly brackets:

}

The If-End clause is now complete, but you need to add an Else clause to give an alternative set of instructions. If the Else clause is left out, the movie clip would never play initially because the _currentframe at the start is less than 10.

4

After the curly bracket you've just added, on the same line add:

else {

5

Add a play action on the next line:

play();

6

Finally, close the else statement with a curly bracket and add a final curly bracket to close the with statement. Your complete code for the second section should look like this:

```
_root.dancer._alpha=66;
with (_root.dancer) {
        if (_currentframe>10) {
        gotoAndPlay (dancer_framelabel);
        } else {
        play();
        };

}
```

STEP 14

rolloverscript:
controlling the logo
MOVIE CLIP

The final section of the RolloverScript controls the title logo, the Logo movie clip that floats briefly across the screen (see figure 08:27). The script itself combines several of the techniques used so far. Here's the section of RolloverScript devoted to the logo contained in the _root.logo object:

```
_root.logo._x=logo_x;
with (_root.manimovie) {
gotoAndPlay("start");
};
```

As you can see, the first line sets the X Position of the object to a variable. Again, the button calling the RolloverScript will supply the value for this variable. The with statement simply plays the specified movie.

figure 08:27

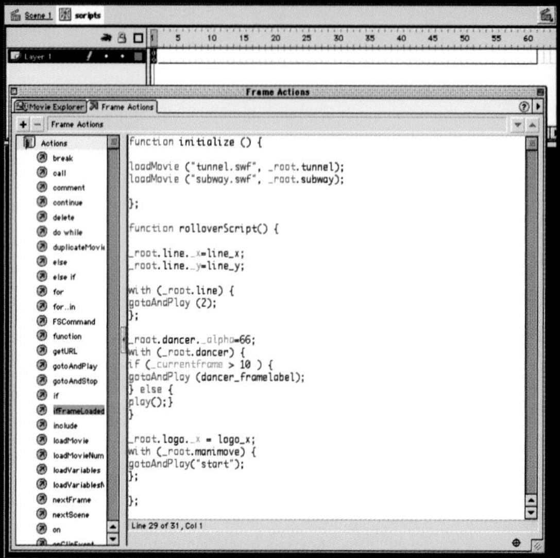

```
function initialize () {

loadMovie ("tunnel.swf", _root.tunnel);
loadMovie ("subway.swf", _root.subway);

};

function rolloverScript() {

_root.line._x=line_x;
_root.line._y=line_y;

with (_root.line) {
gotoAndPlay (2);
};

_root.dancer._alpha=66;
with (_root.dancer) {
if (_currentframe > 10 ) {
gotoAndPlay (dancer_framelabel);
} else {
play();}
}

_root.logo._x = logo_x;
with (_root.manimove) {
gotoAndPlay("start");
};

};
```

Line 29 of 31, Col 1

STEP 15

building the
ROLLOUTSCRIPT

The second generic script called by the various buttons for the ManiFestival is RolloutScript. The RolloutScript implementation is interesting because it shows that you can use variables not only to control properties of an object, such as the X or Y Position, but also to determine which movie is going to be played. The RolloutScript also expands the use of the If-Else-End-If conditional statement.

continues

In RolloutScript, there are two objects that are affected: the larger Subway/Tunnel movie across the top of the stage and the smaller Dancer movie clip. To re-create this script, follow these steps:

1 In our script object, bring up the scripts for our one and only frame by double-clicking on the first frame.

2 Create a new function, this time called rolloutScript:

function rolloutScript() {

}

The first action is to play either the tunnel or the subway movie.

3 With your cursor on the line in between the curly brackets of the rolloutScript function, create the first line of the with statement:

with (whichmovie) {

4 By targeting a variable, whichmovie, instead of a specific movie, each button can now determine the movie clip to be played or otherwise affected.

5 Add a gotoAndPlay action and tell it to goto frame 5. Finally close off the with statement using a curly bracket.

The first part of the RolloutScript is now complete and should look like the example in figure 08:28.

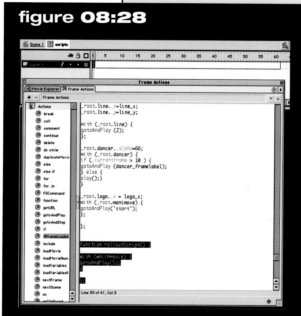

figure 08:28

rolloutscript:
controlling the
DANCER OBJECT

The next part of the script again deals with the _root.dancer object. You want the object to be affected in two ways on rollout: First, it should darken a bit and second, it should stop if one condition is met, otherwise play.

1 After the end of the previous with statement, on the next line set the Alpha property of the Dancer object to 42.

In the previous use of the conditional statement (in the RolloverScript), put an If-Else-End-If clause inside a with statement.

Here, I'll demonstrate another approach—wrapping the conditional statement outside the with actions.

2 Type the following after the previous Alpha setting line:

if (dancer_framelabel=="spin") {

The variable dancer_framelabel will be set by the various buttons; when it is equal to (==) "spin", the following action takes place.

3 Type on the next line:

with (_root.dancer) {

4 On the next line, add:

stop()

5 Close the with statement and then the conditional statement with the appropriate curly brackets:

};
}

6 Following on from the last curly bracket, on the same line add an else statement:

else {

7 On the next line, add a with statement targeting the same dancer clip:

with (_root.dancer) {

8 Add a Play action on the next line. After this, close the with statement and the else statement.

The completed RolloutScript will look like this:

figure **08:29**

```
function rolloutScript() {
        with (whichmovie) {
gotoAndPlay(2);
};
_root.dancer._alpha=42;
if (dancer_framelabel=="spin") {
with (_root.dancer) {
stop();
};
} else {
with (_root.dancer) {
play();
};
};
};
```

adding object-oriented actions to the
NAVIGATION BUTTONS

Now that the generic scripts are built, it is time to add the actions to the various buttons that will call these routines. Each of the three buttons is set up as a symbol and then different actions are added to the instances of those symbols present on the stage. The actions use On mouse events—such as On (Roll Over) and On (Roll Out)—to set variables and trigger the generic action built in the previous section.

about manifestival button

All three of the primary navigation buttons are a similar combination of setting variables and calling scripts. Let's re-create how the About ManiFestival button was set up, with the following steps:

1 Select your button on the stage and then press Ctrl-Alt-A / Cmd-Opt-A to bring up the Object Actions Panel.

2 In the Object Actions Panel, type:

on (rollOver) {

3 We next set three variables:

scripts.line_x = 544;
scripts.line_y = 180;
scripts.dancer_
framelabel = "spin";

In each case, you're setting a variable for the scripts object and then giving it a specific value. With the variables set, you're ready to invoke the routine.

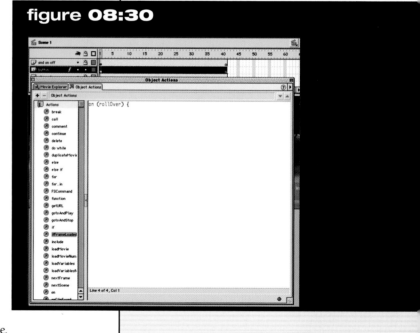

figure 08:30

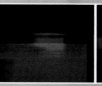

4 On the next line, call the rolloverScript function by adding:

scripts.rolloverScript();

5 Now close the rollover event by adding a curly bracket on the next line, like so:

};

The rollover portion of the action is now done—let's move on to the rollout section.

6 On the next line, add an on rollout event:

on (rollOut) {

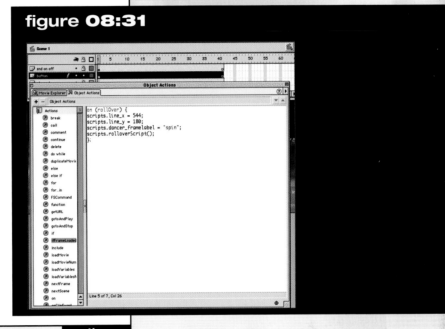

figure **08:31**

continues

7

Set two variables this time, as detailed here:

scripts.whichmovie="_root.subway";
scripts.logo_x = 12;

With these variables, you're setting it up so that the subway movie plays when the user's mouse rolls off this button and the X Position of the logo object is 12 pixels in.

8

On the next line, execute the function by entering:

scripts.rolloutScript();

Here's the completed action for the About the ManiFestival button (see figure 08:32):

figure 08:32

```
on (rollOver) {
scripts.line_x = 544;
scripts.line_y = 180;
scripts.dancer_framelabel = "spin";
scripts.rolloverScript();
};
on (rollOut) {
scripts.whichmovie = "_root.subway";
scripts.logo_x = 12;
scripts.rolloutScript();
};
```

Setting up the other buttons is a similar process. For comparison's sake, here are the two additional scripts:

First, here's the completed action for the About Films button (see figure 08:33):

```
on (rollOver) {
scripts.line_x = 650;
scripts.line_y = 144;
scripts.dancer_framelabel = "one";
scripts.logo_x = 12;
scripts.rolloverScript();
};

on(rollOut) {
scripts.whichmovie = "_root.tunnel";
scripts.logo_x = 12;
scripts.rolloutScript();
};
```

And here's the completed action for the Featured Animation button (see figure 08:34):

```
on (rollOver) {
scripts.line_x = 777;
scripts.line_y = 200;
scripts.dancer_framelabel = "two";
scripts.rolloverScript();
};
```

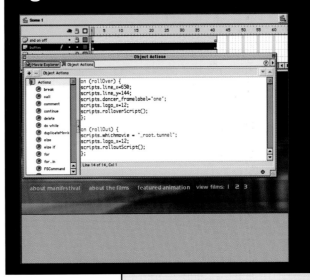

figure 08:33

continues

```
on (rollOut) {
scripts.whichmovie = "nothing";
scripts.logo_x = 12;
scripts.rolloutScript();
};
```

You should recognize most of the variables from the previous section. The only value that may come as a surprise is the one found in the On (Roll Out) section of the Featured Animation movie: "nothing." If you recall, the variable whichmovie is used to determine which movie (I'm nothing if not literal) is played in the generic RolloutScript. Here, "nothing" is not a movie but a simple rectangle graphic. Since you cannot "play" a graphic as you can a movie clip in Flash, no action takes place when whichmovie is set to "nothing."

I've gotten into a lot of detail here for this particular movie. Of the details covered, the following list contains a few major areas:

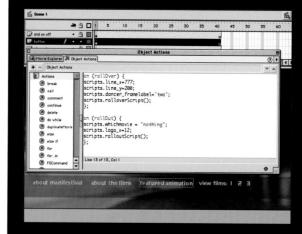

figure **08:34**

- Using the load movie command to load external movies into Target Objects

- The Script object—keeping all of your scripts in once place

- Setting variables

- Using the call action

- Setting variables and using the call command to simulate passing parameters

- Using the If End action

- Using the If End Else action

- Setting properties

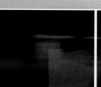

I hope this gives you some insight into Flash 4's ActionScript. I've found it to be simple, elegant, and extremely powerful compared to other scripting languages. Flash 4 gives us all the power to create 2D arcade-like games, interactive multiuser applications, and even entire web sites with only one page of HTML. I hope you can use some of your newly gained knowledge to create your own interactive applications.

And now, back to Hillman...

conclusion

First, let me thank Fred Sharples for this insightful chapter. That said, I must admit that we have a bit of a self-serving angle for including this chapter. What we focus on at hillmancurtis.com is visual communication through motion graphics. So we spend a lot of our time investigating how best to present a client's brand and message. We work hard to identify the essential elements necessary to ensure both a quick-to- download—quick-to-play—file, as well as a consistent and focused message. We are fortunate to have a good client roster and we are kept quite busy designing and implementing motion spots...soooooo, sometimes we lose a bit of our edge on the programming side. Having Fred lay it out like this gets us back in the swing. Flash action scripting is awesome...and seemingly endless in its possibilities. Understanding the principles of OOP, (not to be confused with OPP, the rap song by Naughty by Nature) is essential for working with Flash action scripts.

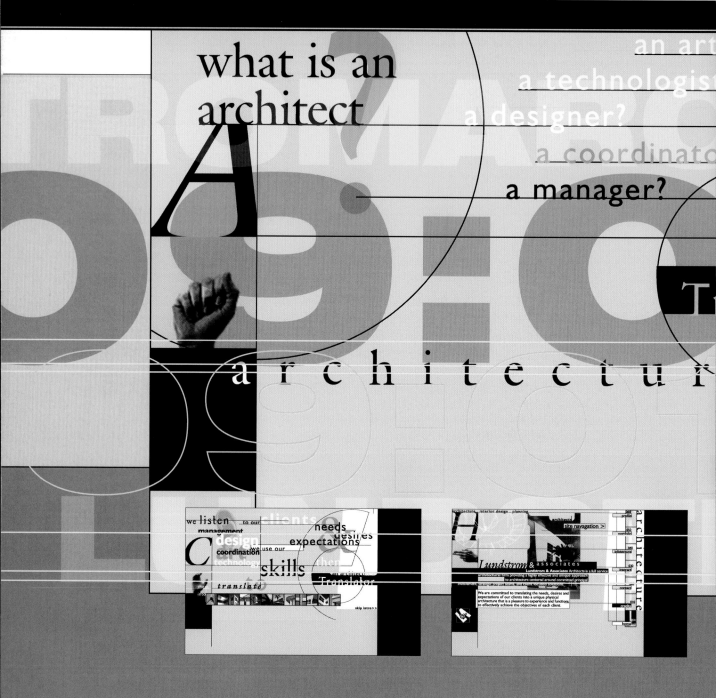

what is an architect

an art
a technologist
a designer?
a coordinato
a manager?

architectur

no!

architect is a

nslator

> "If you want to do great work, you have to be able to generate the great ideas, but, more importantly, be able to sell the great ideas. Many designers struggle with this issue and hope that their work will stand on its own two legs and sell itself. It is not difficult to sell your work if it truly is good and meets the client's objectives; you just need the right tools."

skip intro>>

ARCHITECTURE

BEHIND THE DESIGN

Like many small business, hillmancurtis.com partners with a variety of companies from time to time. One of our most fruitful partnerships has been with Juxt Interactive, a web design and development company based in Newport Beach, California. Juxt outputs some really superb Flash pieces and has developed many techniques worth passing on. One of its most established and far-reaching practices is key for us: getting the business.

Juxt Interactive, and particularly its creative director, Todd Purgason, have developed a method of presenting approaches to a client that is remarkably effective. Even more importantly, its presentation process leads directly into production—significantly smoothing the workflow. Think about the following:

First do creative concepts in an illustration tool, in our case FreeHand 8, take those creative concepts, output them in print form, post them directly to the web, and also be ready to port many of the elements directly into Flash. How cool is that? Your clients get hard copies of your creative concepts and they get the same concepts posted on the web should they need to share with their co-workers in another office…and you have elements from those same concepts that can be imported directly into Flash. Naturally we've ripped off this process, lock, stock, and barrel, from Todd and team and are now in a position to make a hostile takeover bid of Todd's company Juxt Interactive. I'm kidding of course, but the fact remains: Every time we have used the process Todd details in this chapter, we have gotten the job.

I first met Todd Purgason at the 1998 Macromedia User conference. The conference planners had scheduled Todd and me to share a session. I think the session was called "Flash and FreeHand, The Two Amigos." Todd and I spent the couple of hours prior to the session getting to know each other and planning our talk. By the time we were on stage, we had developed a rapport that was natural and the session went great. Later, Todd told me about his company and this process it had developed for winning clients. It may have been the most valuable information I got from the conference and I knew I had to get it into the book.

In this chapter, Todd details this process, which moves from the client presentation developed in FreeHand to production in Flash as exemplified in the deconstruction of one of their award-winning sites, LundstromArts. Take it away, Todd…

print works

Many Flash designers are surprised—and more than a little resistant—when they first hear that our client presentation is print, not screen-based. There's a very good, positive reason for this: Print works. Although it may seem quite literal, we've found that a large-format hard-copy presentation is far more impressive to the client than any comped animation. If you want to do great work, you have to be able to generate the great ideas, but, more importantly, be able to sell the great ideas. Many designers struggle with this issue and hope that their work will stand on its own two legs and sell itself. It is not difficult to sell your work if it truly is good and it meets the client's objectives; you just need the right tools. We have experimented with our clients and have tried different approaches, but the one approach that seems to work without fail, unlike all the others, is large-format presentation boards.

We have come to affectionately call Juxt Interactive's presentation method "the 2×4 approach." It is based on the old idiom "How do you get the attention of a donkey? Hit him over the head with a 2×4." This is not to say that we think of our clients as donkeys, but that we aim to make an impact. We prepare the presentation boards and a well-planned oral presentation, both focused on the goal of exceeding our client's expectations every time. These presentation boards work for us in many ways that screen comps can never achieve. They allow us to control the flow of the discussion as we describe the project that is strategically laid out in moments in time—key pages or keyframes of an animation.

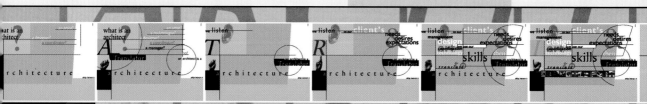

This control allows us to do the following:

- Explain how the client's brand works across the site.

- Show how the site will communicate the client's message to visitors.

- Allow the client time to formulate relevant and intelligent questions.

- Communicate the vision of the piece.

- Clearly communicate what will be delivered.

- Eliminate costly revisions later on in the project.

Figure 09:01 represents a typical 30"×42" presentation board. This particular board was created for a recent project done for Macromedia: the ANDES Coffee storyboard.

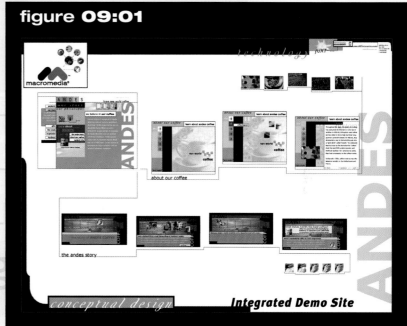

figure 09:01

conceptual design   **Integrated Demo Site**

the pitfalls of screen presentation

Although it may seem like a natural medium for presenting a design concept to a client, the screen has many problems associated with it. First and foremost, this type of presentation is a very time-intensive effort with a limited payoff. It's true that you may be closer to completing the motion graphics, but only if the client accepts the pitch with no changes whatsoever—and the chances of that happening are slim.

Moreover, I find monitor presentations to be ripe targets for disaster. There are so many possibilities for something to go wrong—equipment failure, software failure, network failure, even power failure—that it's a rare demo that proceeds without a hitch. Also, with a screen presentation, the client often finds it more difficult to grasp the entirety of the work, as each moment is presented piece by piece, without an overview or sense of the visual vocabulary.

making an impact and delivering a tangible

By contrast, a big board hard-copy presentation resolves all the monitor issues as well as adding its own advantages. Impact is only half the game; the presence of these large-format presentation pieces communicates to the clients that we have invested a great deal of time and energy to develop their project. The tangible nature of it is nonexistent in a

skip intro>

screen comp, which is often perceived as something that was easy to create and therefore easy to revise, and revise, and revise. The client can touch and hold the printed boards, which gives them a sense of ownership: It is a solid foothold in the mountain they are climbing with us, and it gives them security. If they feel secure they will sit back and let us drive, trusting us as the experts and allowing us to get our job done effectively for us and for them. This security is reinforced during the presentation as we hold the boards and point out key points by physically pointing them out to the clients; nonverbally we are communicating a sense of passion and ownership that we have for the clients' project. The whole point is that we really want to do the best work we can and we work very hard to make sure that there are no barriers keeping us from that goal. Print is just a tool that allows us to communicate the great ideas and, thus, opens the door for us to see them through.

From a conceptual perspective, the clients can more easily see how the design flows across the site and they feel more secure with a tangible. From a practical standpoint, it's far easier to make a major modification—to change a typeface or redesign a layout—at this stage rather than when I'm already animating.

how FreeHand makes this all happen

The amazing thing for us is that the creative assets used in our large-format presentation boards are just a gathering together of sketches created in the conceptualization of the design solution. I have worked in FreeHand for years; it works very well with vector and raster graphics, and I have found it to be an ideal partner to Flash in our development and concepting process. The importance of FreeHand cannot be overemphasized. Although Flash is spectacular at what it does, FreeHand has over 10 years of R&D that was focused on refining the usability and power of its vector-based tools. I can quickly and easily start developing ideas in FreeHand, sketching out concept work that I know can go straight into Flash for animating once the concept is approved. While in FreeHand, I can leverage its powerful typography and illustration tools to quickly get the design from my head to the screen. Most importantly, I am able to use FreeHand's multi-

page tool to lay out moments in time; I can visually study how an animation will work without the time investment of motion effects carried out in Flash at such an early stage. The great thing about it is that when I'm finished sketching and studying the design, I have these great creative assets that can quickly be collected onto a presentation board and outputted for presentation to the clients.

Once the clients have been blown away and have approved the concept, I go back to my FreeHand files knowing that I already have a great head start on production with these assets in FreeHand. FreeHand has a great SWF exporter that takes my layouts into Flash, perfectly preserving my design and automatically creating Flash symbols for optimization in the process.

The way I see it, I don't have two applications with FreeHand and Flash—I have this great development tool that, when effectively leveraged, makes me more creative and more productive, and gives my clients peace of mind.

process overview

To get a better sense of how Juxt Interactive handles the workflow, take a look at this overview of the process:

- **Strategy in FreeHand.** After we've initially met with the clients and done the appropriate analysis of the clients' problem, we develop a strategy and architecture for the project. Using FreeHand, we create the site architecture and interaction diagrams that structurally and functionally illustrate to the clients how the site works and what it consists of.

- **Site design concept.** We focus on creating the key screens or frames—what I refer to as "moments in time." Quite often, I'll create a central moment in time that's at the core of an animation and then work backward and forward from there. It's similar to building your resolve screen first and then making all the steps that lead up to it. However, at this stage, only the most important moments are represented.

- **Presentation boards.** The presentation boards are designed using the assets created during the initial two phases. Because those assets were built with FreeHand, going to print results in high-quality output.

- **Screen layout comps posted to web.** After the clients sign off on the concept, we lay out each page in the entire project and export the pages from FreeHand as JPEGs. These JPEGs are posted to our development extranet for the clients to review and approve.

- **SWF export.** The FreeHand comps are exported as SWF files in stages to retain backgrounds and foreground elements, as well as text blocks and text as paths.

- **Animation and interactivity.** In Flash, animation and interactivity are added to the static imported images. Each moment in time is treated like a keyframe and additional frames are tweened and created as needed.

- **Promotion.** We typically return to the original FreeHand layouts to leverage creative assets to be used in print-based promotional pieces for the project.

STEP 01

deconstructing LundstromARCH

The LundstromARCH project illustrates how this design process is actualized. Lundstrom & Associates is a small architectural firm in southern California specializing in high-tech "smart classrooms" and university buildings (see figure 09:02). The challenge of this project was to convey Lundstrom's technological capabilities to university architects, a market segment that exhibits unusually high design standards.

The site was designed to communicate two messages. First, through visual design and content it communicates that, no matter what type of project the firm is working on, Lundstrom & Associates is concerned with listening to the needs of its clients. Second, Lundstrom is presented as technologically savvy, a quality that is essential to developing "smart classrooms."

To get across the idea that Lundstrom—as an example of the best kind of architect—was always attuned to its clients' needs, we came up with the concept of the translator. A translator is always listening and his job, in essence, is to react to what he hears. The very use of our web site medium, Flash, marked Lundstrom as technologically savvy while being capable of sophisticated design imagery.

figure 09:02

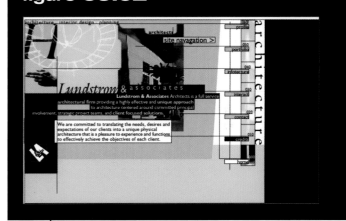

skip intro>

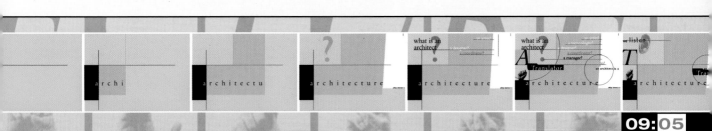

sketching the intro ANIMATION

With our concept firmly in place, it's time to begin sketching ideas for the introductory animation. The goal of the first sketch is to lay out the first, key moment in time; the resulting initial FreeHand page is shown in figure 09:03. Each of the elements on the page—text and graphic—has the potential for movement that will eventually be realized in Flash. Moreover, the first sketch also begins to establish the palette and style.

With the first moment in time realized, the next step is to duplicate the page in FreeHand both forward and backward. In other words, the page is now duplicated twice. With three identical pages, the second page will remain as is and modifications will be made to page 1 and page 3. On page 1, many foreground elements will be removed, and only the background and a key symbol or two will remain, as shown in figure 09:04. On page 3, existing elements from our first moment in time will be enhanced; new elements will be introduced while a few objects are carried over (see figure 09:05). Now the intro is beginning to take shape with three of the primary moments in time.

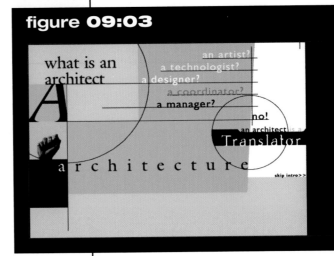

figure 09:03

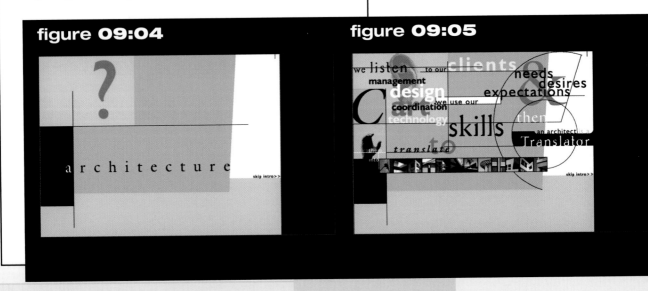

figure 09:04

figure 09:05

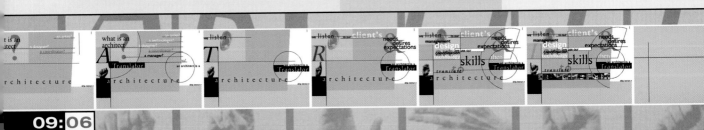

figure 09:06

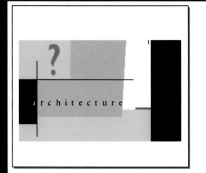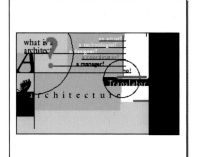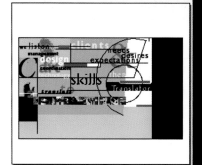

Once a number of pages are developed, it's time to step back and study the progression of the design. With FreeHand's paged layout system, that's simply a matter of zooming out; in this case, going to 25% allows me to see the first three pages, as shown in figure 09:06. I look for a consistency of approach and flow of design here. It's also a good time for experimentation. I like to duplicate pages and make alterations and modifications to see what develops—this experimentation is far easier at this stage of the game than it would be if I had developed the early concept in Flash.

skip intro>>

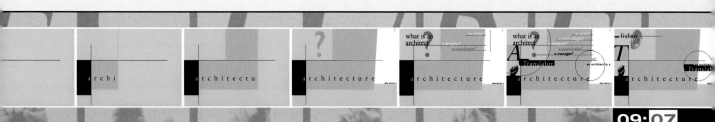

the concept
DESIGN BOARD

After a final design has been arrived at, the sketches are brought together for output on a presentation board. This is a fairly straightforward process in FreeHand and also allows for another print opportunity: handouts for the clients. Although the large format presentation board is the clients' primary focus, handouts—derived from the page layouts done in FreeHand—offer a reference that can be reviewed at a later time.

We put a lot of work into the design itself and into selling the design. The goal is to overwhelm the clients with the quality and thoroughness of the presentation. Most of the time, we exceed the clients' expectations and earn their trust and confidence.

Figure 09:07 shows an example of the large format presentation board that we use.

figure **09:07**

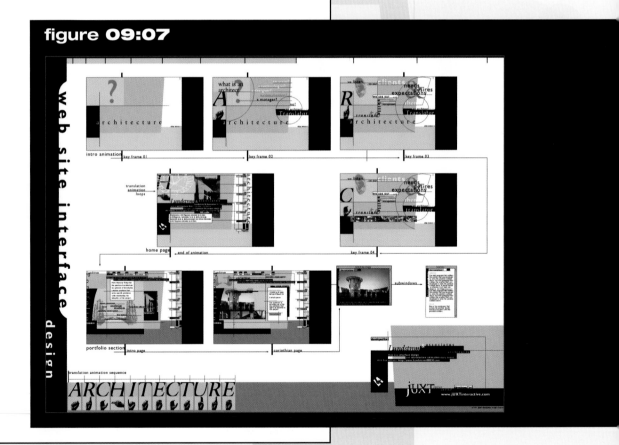

moving from FreeHand
TO FLASH

One of the key advantages of sketching your initial designs in FreeHand is its capability to export to Flash with remarkable f idelity. The vast majority of your objects in FreeHand become identical assets in Flash, especially since the release of FreeHand 8.01. This version of the program offers increased—almost intelligent—SWF export control. By adhering to a few simple rules, you can easily adapt your static images in FreeHand into Flash animated ones.

With FreeHand 8.01, you can export to Flash an entire image or selected objects only. I'll typically perform an export in two stages, one for objects with text as paths and one for text blocks to retain the leading and other text features. TIFF images—which we often integrate in our vector graphics—are automatically converted to RGB format during export.

Perhaps best of all, each separate object, whether used for the background or the foreground, is brought in as a separate object positioned exactly as in FreeHand. This translation allows ultimate flexibility for animation possibilities in Flash. Background objects can remain static and foreground objects can animate into place; or, if I choose, some background objects can also move into position over time.

To better understand the FreeHand-to-Flash export connection, follow these steps:

1   In FreeHand, select all the elements on the first page you want to export, and copy them.

2   Open a new page by choosing File > New.

3   Paste the elements onto the new page, snapping them into the upper-left corner.

With the page isolated—and the original design safe—we can separate the text to be converted to paths from the text to be exported as text blocks.

4   Create a new layer.

continues

skip intro >>

5 Select all the text elements that you wish to retain as text blocks and cut them.

6 Select the new layer and lock all others.

7 Paste the cut text blocks into the new layer.

8 Hide the text block layer and unlock the other layers.

9 Select File > Export and change the file type on the Export Document dialog to Flash (*.swf).

10 Select Setup.

The Flash Export dialog, shown in figure 09:08, is displayed.

11 Set both Path Compression and Image Compression to None.

You want the highest fidelity for your paths and images.

12 In the Text list, choose Convert to Paths.

13 Unless you are animating layers or pages, deselect those options and click OK when you're ready.

14 Enter a filename and path for the Flash file in the Export Document dialog.

15 In the Layers inspector, display the text block layer and hide all others.

16 Repeat steps 9–15, with one exception: Change the Text option to Maintain Blocks (see figure 09:09).

17 Enter a new name for the text block file to complete the export.

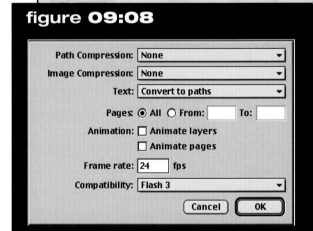

figure 09:08

Path Compression:	None
Image Compression:	None
Text:	Convert to paths
Pages:	● All ○ From: [ ] To: [ ]
Animation:	☐ Animate layers
	☐ Animate pages
Frame rate:	24 fps
Compatibility:	Flash 3

Cancel   OK

figure 09:09

Path Compression:	None
Image Compression:	None
Text:	Maintain blocks
Pages:	● All ○ From: [ ] To: [ ]
Animation:	☐ Animate layers
	☐ Animate pages
Frame rate:	30 fps
Compatibility:	Flash 3

Cancel   OK

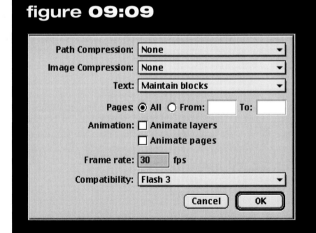

setting up FreeHand
COLORS TO
EXPORT TO FLASH

It is critical that you set up the FreeHand preferences correctly to get web-safe colors from FreeHand design layouts to Flash. First you need to set the export color mode to RGB (see figure 09:10). Next, you need to be sure to turn all color management off (see figure 09:11). If you fail to set this up correctly, you will get unpredictable export results or no export at all.

figure 09:10

figure 09:11

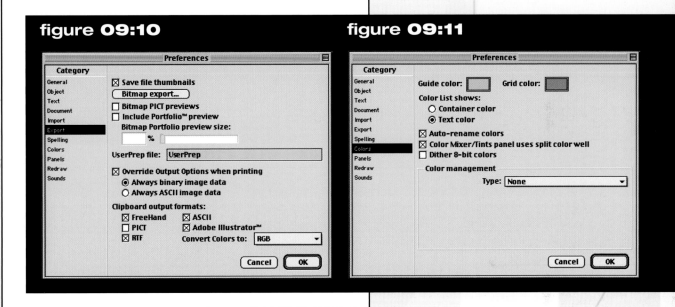

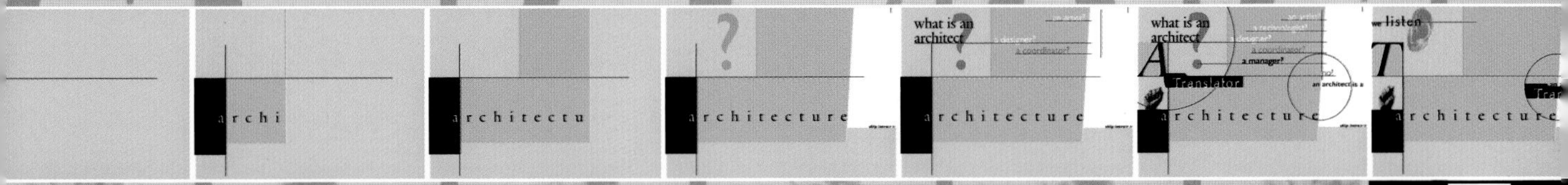

organizing imported
OBJECTS

The flip side of any export operation is importing. Although the actual importing is handled in a one-step command (File > Import), there are a few things you need to know about importing complex work from FreeHand to make the most of it in Flash.

- It is very important that you set your movie options in the beginning to match the size of your layout from FreeHand (see figure 09:12).

- FreeHand tends to create nested groups of objects which, in most cases, need to be broken apart to be truly useful.

- FreeHand breaks apart text boxes line by line. In such a circumstance, the best course would be to import only the first line of text as a placeholder. Then, simply copy the text content from the FreeHand text block and paste it into the text block in Flash.

- Clipping paths are handled differently in FreeHand than in Flash. In FreeHand, a clipping path is one object with another pasted inside of it. In Flash, the clipping is composed of an outline and separate transparent fill that you need to move out of the way to get to the object inside.

- As noted earlier, TIFFs are converted to RGB images. If the image is colorized in FreeHand, Flash applies the color settings; if it's a black-and-white TIFF set to transparent, Flash automatically brings in the alpha channel.

After I have imported the exported SWF files (one for text blocks and one for text paths), I organize the file. I systematically take all the objects and move them to their own layers, converting each object into a symbol. I tend to use the Paste in Place feature as I move objects to their own layer, thus retaining the original positioning. Admittedly this is a fairly tedious process, but one that reaps tremendous rewards (see figure 09:13).

figure 09:12

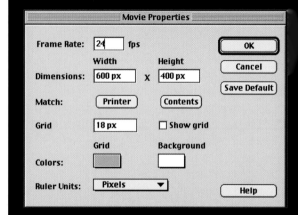

figure 09:13

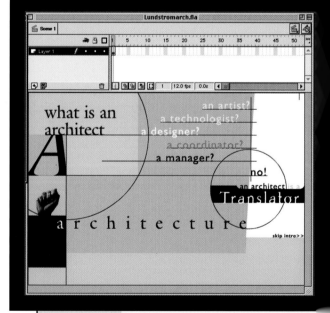

executing the ANIMATION

Now, with my initial moment in time in Flash and set up appropriately, it's time to begin executing the animation. At this stage, I tend to work with FreeHand and Flash side by side, either exporting small objects I find I need, or copying and pasting them.

My process is straightforward. I first hide all the layers in Flash, except for the background and the first object, which I refer to as a cast member. Then, I develop its motion or its tween and place it down the Timeline. Then, I turn on the layer for the next cast member I want to appear and follow the same procedure: Develop its motion or tween, move it further down the Timeline, and remove its earlier appearance. I repeat this process for each of the cast members until the first moment in time is completely revealed. Figure 09:14 shows a partially developed Flash movie where the background layer is in place, and the initial key elements have begun to appear.

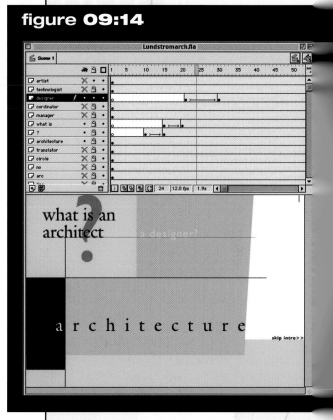

figure **09:14**

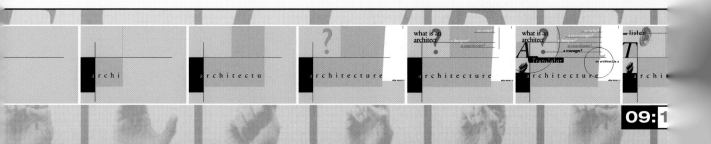

importing the next
MOMENT IN TIME

In the LundstromARCH project, the next moment in time to import is a more complex version of the previous page. Many elements, such as the background and certain cast members, are common to both. Rather than import redundant elements and have to delete them in Flash, I remove them prior to exporting.

Maintaining the alignment of objects is not a problem as long as you consistently follow the same procedure:

1 Select and copy all the needed objects.

2 Create a new page and paste the copied objects, snapping them into the upper-left corner.

After deleting the redundant elements and exporting, I import them into a working layer in Flash (see figure 09:15). Then, I follow the same process of organizing the new objects into their own layers, symbolizing them and then moving each into its proper position on the Timeline. If necessary, transitions are added between the existing and the new elements.

Not every object coming out of FreeHand needs to be exported as an SWF file. For many smaller cast members, copying the object in FreeHand and pasting in Flash works perfectly well. Some Macintosh users have complained that the copy-and-paste method does not work for them; there appears to be a conflict on certain systems with this operation and the Mac desktop. If the icons are moved off the desktop, the copy and paste works as expected.

figure 09:15

The guide layer capabilities in Flash are very useful in a copy-and-paste scenario. Because the exact positioning of your elements in FreeHand is no longer available for a pasted object, an alternative placement method must be used. With my newly pasted object on its own layer, Alt-click the guide symbol for the object's layer. This displays every other layer, except the current one, as a guide and greatly simplifies placement (see figure 09:16).

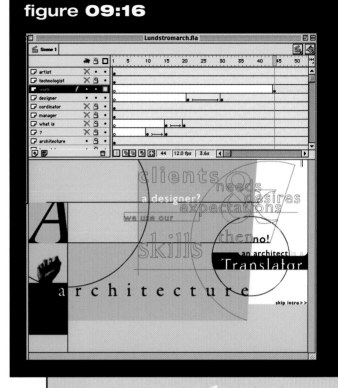

figure 09:16

legacy

Developing your Flash assets in FreeHand or other vector-based illustration tool brings what we refer to as *legacy* to the table. With legacy in hand, new material can be more quickly created. Everything from an HTML sister site—developed with Macromedia's Fireworks—to promotional materials are much easier to create out of the assets generated by FreeHand (see figure 09:17). These future spin-off projects are perhaps the biggest win we receive from using FreeHand. Such spin-offs are good for our company financially especially because the legacy assets are in place. Anyone who has tried to get viable assets out of Flash knows that the process is far more difficult.

figure 09:17

conclusion

Keep in mind that I'm not advocating the total replacement of Flash's creative tools with those of FreeHand or any other vector-based illustration tool—I am, rather, playing to each tool's strength and taking advantage of its strong interconnection. FreeHand has 10 years of R&D behind it, making it a very creative, flexible illustration tool. Although many of the effects possible in FreeHand can be replicated in Flash, many would take much more effort and time.

In summary, FreeHand or other vector-based illustration tools give you a number of advantages that Flash alone does not afford:

- A powerful and quick design space for developing ideas and studying them over time.

- Presentation boards that allow you to strategically communicate your design intent to the clients.

- The deliverables necessary to give the clients security in understanding where the project is going.

- A safe presentation environment that is free from any technological hiccups.

- A powerful production environment that allows you to quickly study and realize your project.

- A strategic process that sets you up to cost effectively develop additional work for the client in the future.

I have tried to shed light on a working situation that works with your Flash skillset to empower you to be a better designer and a better communicator. When you bring a tool like FreeHand or another vector-based illustration application that allows you to output print, you can tap into a fast, flexible, and effective development process. Most importantly, you have the tools you need to present and sell your Flash designs to clients without spending the entire budget just to get the approval to proceed. Large output storyboards have been a key factor in the success of Juxt Interactive and they have allowed us to push our design envelope, giving us more creative freedom. I think that is the bottom line for us designers; if we are going to do lame design, we would be better off as postmen. So why not empower your design projects with the tools necessary to sell that great idea to the clients (without going broke in the process) and giving yourself opportunity to expand the scope of services at the same time.

skip intro>

Resources

10:10:10

> "Let's talk about resources here. I have a bunch of sites that I consult all the time. Some are straight-up techie sites, others are design sites...Flash design, video, movie trailers...what have you. I have a list of great books as well."

inspirational Flash SITES

Design in Motion
http://www.designinmotion.com

This site, presented by the Broadcaster Designers Association, is a plethora of motion graphics inspiration. See the latest broadcast spots, film trailers, and video for the web. Solid interviews with the designers...pretty good technical info.

RSUB
http://www.rsub.com

Craig, Carah, Hillary, Michael, and company keep this site at the top of my list. It's creative, inspiring, and subversive all at once. There's something here for everyone. I like the sections rsubox (streaming DV shorts), typographic (a beautiful interactive look into typography), and disinformation the best.

Born Magazine
http://www.bornmag.com

Web design and literature. Done right.

KALIBER 10000
http://www.kaliber10000.net/

Good looking and smart...plenty of design news and links.

Design Agency
http://www.design-agency.com/

This is a portal of sorts, showcasing new design talent.

Twenty2Product
http://www.twenty2.com/

I know Terry through e-mails, and he seems like a nice guy... the work he does with his wife is exceptional and inspiring.

Imaginary Forces
http://www.imaginaryforces.com

The legendary Kyle Cooper's company. This is the guy who got me really into motion graphics. His site has good examples of his huge body of work.

415
http://www.415.com

My old pals from San Francisco. They are really clever with concepts, and they just keep growing and cranking out the good work.

Bionic Arts
http://www.bionicarts.com

Damn...

Shift
http://www.shift.jp.org

One of my favorites. A site dedicated to inspirational design and designers.

RESMAG
http://www.resmag.com

Just visit this site to subscribe to this exceptional DV magazine.

Digitalthread
http://www.digitalthread.com

This is another great site that showcases new work from designers all over the world.

Volumeone
http://www.volumeone.com

Matt Owens is a design freak. He's a brother from another planet with this stuff...if you know what I mean. Great inspiration. Great guy.

Lynda Weinman
http://www.lynda.com

Lynda is simply the best teacher out there...her site is a great resource.

Saul Bass on the Web

http://www.saulbass.com

These folks from the U.K. have put together a killer site on the master and, some could argue, the originator of motion graphics, Saul Bass.

Akimbo Design

http://www.akimbo.com

Ardith Ibañez and Ben Rigby have a good thing going here. Great designer married to a super programmer.

JUXT Interactive

http://www.juxtinteractive.com

Todd Purgason wrote Chapter 9 in this book, so you have probably seen some of his work and don't need me to tell you how beautiful it is. Check out his company site…there's always new stuff, new inspiration.

Orange Design

http://www.orangedesign.com

Fred Sharples wrote Chapter 8 in this book. He and his wife, Pam, cannot be touched for designing deeply interactive Flash sites and advertisements. Very simply the best at Flash programming.

technical Flash sites

Colin Moock

http://www.moock.org

First and foremost, is my little homie Colin Moock. He's not really my "little homie," since I have never actually met Colin. Still, his site has definitely "got my back" more than once. (I'm listening to the late, great Tupac now, which explains the tone of this entry.) This is the best Flash troubleshooting and programming site around. I don't know how he does it, but every time I run into a problem…like, how to launch a sized browser from Flash, or how to close a browser from Flash, or how to check for the Flash plug-in without using Java…I go to moock.org and the solution is there. Not only does Colin explain things in a clear and comprehendible way, he actually has source files there for download. Priceless.

Flash Kit

http://www.flashkit.com

Excellent site here. These guys have a ton of downloadable files, tutorials, sound loops, and whatnot. Plus they have a link out to the Hunger Site. Hats off!

FlashLite

http://www.flashlite.net/

Again, a site with plenty of useful Flash 4 tips and techniques.

FlashZone

http://www.flashzone.com/

Cool stuff here. A great all-around resource for everything Flash.

Macromedia

http://www.macromedia.com/support/flash/

Of course the Macromedia site offers great tutorials, technotes, and links to developers.

audio loops and SOFTWARE

loopZ

http://www.loopz.com

A dollar a loop at this site. And the loops are good. I've used several in my work. Easy to find, updated often…all in all, a great resource for tight, small, clean audio loops.

WavCentral

http://www.wavcentral.com

Free effects and loops.

XS4ALL

http://xs4all.dk/products.shtml

Makes a very cool MP3-to-WAV application. That way you can go to mp3.com, grab a cool sound, and turn it into a .wav file for use in Flash.

Winamp

http://www.winamp.com

MP3 player that also allows you to decode from MP3 to WAV/AIF.

Sonic Foundry

http://www.sonicfoundry.com

Makers of SoundForge wave edit software and Acid loop-based music production tools.

stats sites

StatMarket

http://www.statmarket.com/

A good site to send your clients to when they ask about player install base…and anything else out there. But now it's going to cost you about a grand a year. Still, we might do it, just because they were so damn good when they were a free service.

TheCounter.com

http://www.thecounter.com/

Pretty good all around stats…no stats on players, though, last I checked. It's free.

Macromedia

http://www.macromedia.com/
software/player_census/sources.html

This is Macromedia's player download/install base stats page.

recommended books

There are so many great design books coming out all the time. Here are a few that have helped and inspired me.

Tibor Kalman: Perverse Optimist
by Tibor Kalman, et al.

Before I bought this book, its vibe kind of bugged me… I don't know, maybe the cover, maybe the feeling of "members only" that I sometimes get around the NYC design community who's who…whatever. But let me say that I regret waiting so long to buy it. This man Tibor Kalman didn't really design "pretty pictures" …he designed brilliant concepts, commentaries, ideas, inspirations, provocations, and subversions. This book is packed with so many amazing ideas from Tibor and his company M&Co, it makes my heart beat a little faster every time I open it. Not without its contradictions and annoyances, but anyone willing to push envelopes this way is willing to make a fool of himself. I hope one day to have this kind of courage.

Fotografiks
by David Carson and Phillip B. Meggs

I know a lot of designers who don't have much good to say about Carson, but like him or not, he's a major innovator. His work is everywhere and has inspired every designer I know, at some point or another. This book is beautiful; I draw inspiration from it constantly.

Designagent Km7: License to Design
by Klaus Mai, et al.

Great book for us Flash and FreeHand/Illustrator vector people. Great style and plenty of inspiration. I consult this book for ideas all the time.

I Am Almost Always Hungry
by Abraham Cahan

Well…way back when I was just hired as a contractor at Macromedia I was invited, for some reason, to the offices of Cahan and Associates to discuss the annual report they were designing for Macromedia. At the time, I could barely grasp the concept of e-mail, let alone corporate design, so I just sat there intimidated and silent. But I was so impressed by the process I witnessed that I decided to follow this firm's work…and I was psyched to see this book out. I bought it immediately and have not been disappointed.

Type in Motion: Innovations in Digital Graphics
by Jeff Bellantoni and Matt Woolman

This is a book I sent to Todd Purgason when he agreed, thank God, to design my book. Beautiful motion graphics work displayed in a beautiful and inspiring way.

Bill Viola
by David A. Ross, et al.

Bill Viola is a video artist hero of mine. If you get a chance to see any of his work you should not miss the opportunity. This book is visually stimulating, but it's a book that I can read like a good novel. The interviews with Viola are wonderful, his concepts and inspirations are revealed, and the resulting work suddenly glows with new meaning.

Paul Rand
by Steven Heller, et al.

Like Saul Bass, Paul Rand represents a major figure in graphic design. The body of work displayed in this book is awe-inspiring.

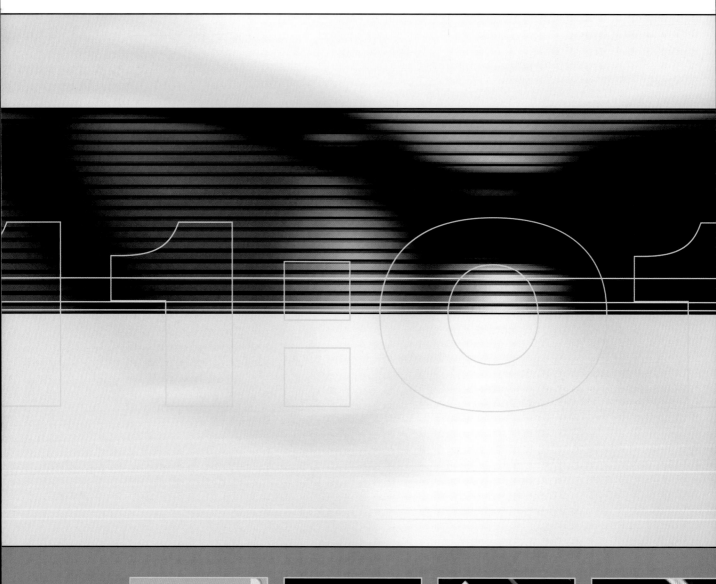

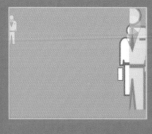

Sound.

WE SAY: IT'S HERE, CLOSER THAN YOU THINK

macromedia SHOCK(z)

P

Q–R

U–V

W–Z

WE SAY: IT'S HERE, CLOSER THAN YOU THINK

Sound.

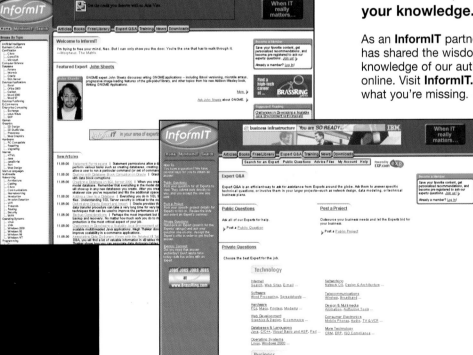

Flash Web Design is brought to you by...

Hillman Curtis

Hillman Curtis, principal and creative director of hillmancurtis.com, inc. a design firm in New York City, represents the cutting edge of motion graphic design on the Web today. His expert and innovative use of Flash 4 has garnered him the Communication Arts Award of Excellence, the One Show gold, New Media Invision Bronze, and the South by Southwest Conference "Best Use of Design" and "Best of Show"; hillmancurtis.com is a How magazine Top 10 web site. Hillman's work is featured in major design magazines and books, and his reputation continues to grow around the world. Hillman has appeared as a speaker at design conferences in Japan, Paris, New York, San Francisco, Chicago, and Atlanta. His company's current client roster includes Intel, Iomega, 3Com, Hewlett Packard, DSW partners, Ogilvy One, Goodby Silverstein & Partners, SonicNet, Macromedia, Capitol Records, Lycos, WebTV, Sun, and others. Hillman also acts as a strategic advisor to Razorfish.

David Baldeschwieler

David Baldeschwieler is the technical media designer for Macromedia's marketing team, where he designs and produces live product demos and marketing materials for the company's full suite of 11 web publishing products. David began his graphic design career in 1994 before earning his BFA from the University of the Pacific in 1996. David's career took an unexpected turn in 1997 when he began working as Software Quality Assurance Engineer on a product called Macromedia Flash. As a key member of the development team, he helped spec, test, and ship Flash 2, 3, and 4. David has helped to write and produce Lynda Weinman's "Learning Flash 4.0" video series, and demonstrated and trained Flash authoring techniques at the Macromedia Users Conference '97, the Ojai Digital Arts Center, the San Francisco Macromedia User's Forum, the San Francisco Academy of Art, MacWorld, and Seybold.

Brendan Dawes

Brendan is an interactive designer whose portfolio includes work for Disney, Golden Wonder, Club 18-30, Volvic, Fox Kids, Kelloggs, and Coca-Cola Schweppes. As well as commercial work, Bren also has personal projects including the highly acclaimed Saul Bass web site, and its quirky offshoot, Psycho Studio, an application built entirely in Flash that allows you to edit your own version of the Psycho shower scene! It was in fact through the Saul Bass site that Bren and Hillman's paths crossed back in 1999 at the Macromedia European UCON in Paris. Over the years, Brendan's work has been featured in many industry publications and books and received various awards, including three Shockwave Sites Of The Day and a nomination in the New York Flash Film Festival. He also writes Dreamweaver extensions and wrote the official QuickTime extension in conjunction with Apple and Macromedia.

Ian Kovalik

As art director for Hillmancurtis.com, inc., Ian Kovalik has designed or directed motion spots for clients such as Intel, 3com, Lotus, WebTV, Lycos, Macromedia, Iomega, SonicNet, Razorfish, Ogilvy One, DSW Partners, and Goodby Silverstein and Partners. Along with his expertise in motion design (2D and 3D), Ian brings to Hillmancurtis.com an interest in traditional illustration, graphic design, and video cinematography. When not in the office, he can be found in his East Village loft writing or illustrating his upcoming children's book. Ian holds a bachelor's degree from Boston College, design credits from Parson's School of Design in NYC, and an incredible debt to his mother and father.